CAMBER

BOOKS BY DON McKAY

POETRY

Air Occupies Space   1973

Long Sault   1975

Lependu   1978

Lightning Ball Bait   1980

Birding, or desire   1983

Sanding Down This Rocking Chair on a Windy Night   1987

Night Field   1991

Apparatus   1997

Another Gravity   2000

Camber: Selected Poems 1983-2000   2004

Strike/Slip   2006

ESSAYS

Vis à vis: Fieldnotes on Poetry and Wilderness   2001

Deactivated West 100   2005

CAMBER

Selected Poems 1983-2000

DON McKAY

McCLELLAND & STEWART

LIBRARY AND ARCHIVES CANADA CATALOGUING IN PUBLICATION

McKay, Don, 1942-
Camber : selected poems, 1983-2000 / Don McKay.

ISBN 978-0-7710-5765-6

I. Title.

PS8575.K28A6 2004   C811'.54   C2003-906866-8

We acknowledge the financial support of the Government of Canada
through the Book Publishing Industry Development Program and that of
the Government of Ontario through the Ontario Media Development
Corporation's Ontario Book Initiative. We further acknowledge the support
of the Canada Council for the Arts and the Ontario Arts Council for our
publishing program.

Typeset in Aldus by M&S, Toronto
Printed and bound in Canada

ANCIENT FOREST
FRIENDLY

McClelland & Stewart Ltd.
75 Sherbourne Street
Toronto, Ontario
M5A 2P9
www.mcclelland.com

3 4 5 6 7   11 10 09 08 07

TABLE OF CONTENTS

III *Night Field*

IV *Apparatus*

V *Another Gravity*

Lifting off, letting go, seizing leave as though
departure were the first act ever, stepping
into air as sigh, as outbreath, hum,
commotion, whirr,
it's out of here, it's shucked us like
high school, like some stiff
chrysalis it lets fall from invisible
unfolding wings.
                    And already we are saying
let there be, let there be
liftoff, let there be loss, let there be those
silver knives that swim in blood like sharpened
fingerlings, those tossed-off
warbler phrases that dissolve in air before
the voice can manage to corral them, that exquisite thirst
whose satisfaction is another,
larger thirst equipped with claws like question marks requiring
answers in the form of still another thirst and
though we recognize this evil as our own we also
recognize the camber of its nothing as it
lifts, as it glances,
as it vanishes.

I

FIELD MARKS

Distinguished from the twerp,
which he resembles, by his off-speed
concentration: *shh:*
                    bursting with sneakiness
he will tiptoe through our early morning drowse
like the villain in an old cartoon, pick up
binoculars, bird book, dog,
orange, letting the fridge lips close behind him with a kiss.
Everything,
even the station-wagon, will be
delicate with dew –
bindweed, spiderweb, sumac,
Queen Anne's lace: he slides
among them as a wish, attempting to become
a dog's nose of receptiveness.

Later on he'll come back as the well-known bore
and read his list (Song sparrows: 5
                    Brown thrashers: 2
                    Black-throated green warblers: 1)   omitting
  all the secret data hatching on the far side of his mind:

              that birds have sinuses throughout their bodies,
              and that their bones are flutes
              that soaring turkey vultures can detect
                            depression and careless driving
              that every feather is a pen, but living,

              flying

CLOSE-UP ON A SHARP-SHINNED HAWK

Concentrate upon her attributes:
the accipiter's short
rounded wings, streaked breast, talons fine
and slender as the x-ray of a baby's hand.
The eyes (yellow in this hatchling
later deepening to orange then
blood red) can spot
a sparrow at four hundred metres and impose
silence like an overwhelming noise
to which you must not listen.

Suddenly, if you're not careful, everything
goes celluloid and slow
and threatens to burn through and you
must focus quickly on the simple metal band around her leg
by which she's married to our need to know.

THE GREAT BLUE HERON

What I remember
about the Great Blue Heron that rose
like its name over the marsh
is touching and holding that small
manyveined
wrist
upon the gunwale, to signal silently –

                       look

The Great Blue Heron
(the birdboned wrist).

DUSK:

the slow
rollover of evening, the spruce
growing dense, gathering dark,
standing in pools of departure.

Take care . . . Remember . . .
we are weaving a wreath of human hair
to be left to the Huron County Museum
with a short note saying who
contributed and where they come from.

Shadows sadden.
The details of your face escape like minnows.
We become weight –

until the balance tips entirely and a bat
breaks out like a butterfly's subconscious flashing,
dancing his own black rag.

I SCREAM YOU SCREAM

Waking JESUS sudden riding a scream like a
train braking metal on metal on
metal teeth receiving signals from a dying star sparking
off involuntarily in terror in all directions in the
abstract incognito in my
maidenform bra in an expanding universe in a where's
my syntax thrashing
loose like a grab that like a
look out like a
live wire in a hurricane until

until I finally tie it down:
it is a pig scream
a pig scream from the farm across the road
that tears this throat of noise into the otherwise anonymous dark,
a noise not oink or grunt
but a passage blasted through constricted pipes, perhaps
a preview of the pig's last noise.

Gathering again toward sleep I sense
earth's claim on the pig.
Pig grew, polyped out on the earth like a boil
and broke away.
                            But earth
heals all flesh back beginning with her pig,
filling his throat with silt and sending
subtle fingers for him like the meshing fibres in a wound
like roots

like grass growing on a grave like a snooze
in the sun like fur-lined boots that seize
the feet like his *nostalgie de la boue* like
having another glass of booze like a necktie like a
velvet noose like a nurse

like sleep.

NOCTURNAL ANIMALS

Another cup of coffee. Southern Ontario
surrounds this kitchen like well-fed flesh.
If I had
a cigarette right now I'd smoke it like an angry campfire
burn it into the unblemished body of the night.

Lonely is a knife whose handle fits the mind
too well, its oldest and most hospitable friend.
On Highway 22
a truck is howling for Sarnia or London.
In my garage
the aging Buick is dreaming the commercial
in which he frees my spirit into speed while an eagle
                    in slow motion
beats applause above our heads.

Another cup of coffee.
Two years ago the wolves took shape
in Lobo Township, lifting the tombstone of its name
to lope across these snowy fields
                                    between the woodlots
                        spectral
                                    legless as wind, their nostrils
wide with news of an automated pig barn
waiting for them like an all-night restaurant.

Shot, their bodies wisped away, their eyes
stubbed out.

FRIDGE NOCTURNE

When it is late, and sleep,
off somewhere tinkering with his motorcycle, leaves you
locked in your iron birdhouse,
listen to your fridge, the old
armless weeping willow of the kitchen.

Humble murmur, it works its way
like the river you're far from, the Saugeen, the Goulais
the Raisin
muddily gathers itself in pools to drop things in
and fish things from,
the goodwill mission in the city of dreadful night.

Remembering: the annual Community Chest Christmas Concert. Phone in your request with a donation, listen in bed to hear it on the radio, the small moon of the dial an extra presence in the dark as we gather toward Christmas. Jokes about the police chief and the high-school principals. Choirs, bands, Billy Heward played White Christmas on the trumpet. Was it the same year someone (who?) paid twenty dollars to hear my father, a lapsed Kinsman, de da de dum his way through the Kinsmen Friendship Song while I lay thrilled and mortified *yer old man never even knew the tune let alone the words?* Might have been. At any rate I recall my father telling the story of the bird flying around the high school auditorium, fluttering wildly overhead and distracting the audience from the Ecole Immaculée Conception choir singing Frosty the Snowman. By the time the Gilbert and Sullivan star tenor took the stage the bird (sparrow? hummingbird? Blackburnian warbler?) had extended its range to buzz performers. George would be singing something Irish, his voice clenched, his face set in the abstract concentration of a constipated man, while I see the bird flashing into the spotlight, homing on this rope of sinew in the air and veering away each time just before he flies down George's throat. The story goes that George dropped not one note nor lost an ounce of poise as he caught the bird in one hand, squeezing it to death while he launched into his climax. The story leaves me lying in the dark trying to imagine how a voice might swell with heartbeats, break, and fly away, beyond the reach of radio.

Later – My father now says:

> that the concert was the Kinsmen Festival of Stars
>
> that the singer was fourteen-year-old Vincent Delasio
>
> that the song was O for the Wings of a Dove
>
> that the bird was a bat
>
> that Vincent Delasio caught the bat on his third
> attempt and held it until it bit him, then flung
> it to the floor in pain and fury, and that later
> he was persuaded to return, bandaged, and sang
> again to thunderous applause.

My father will not say whether the bat survived.

THE BOY'S OWN GUIDE TO DREAM BIRDS

Audubonless
dream birds thrive. The talking swan, the kestrels
nesting in the kitchen, undocumented citizens of teeming
terra incognita.
                    To write
their book the boy will need
la plume de ma tante, harfang des neiges,
patience, an ear like a cornucopia, and at least
an elementary understanding of the place of human psychology
among nature's interlocking food chains.
                                        For the facts are scarce
and secretive. Who is able to identify
the man in metamorphosis, becoming
half-bird on the Coldstream Road? The boy reports
a falcon's beak both hooked and toothed, the fingers spreading,
lengthening into a vulture's fringe, the cold eye
glaring as he lifts off from the road: look, look,
come quick!
            Who sits inside and fails to hear?
            What can he be doing?
            Why is he so deaf?

But on another night a huge, hunched, crested
multicoloured bird, a sort of cross between eagle
and macaw, sits, sinister and gorgeous,
on our mailbox.
Now we know what happens to the letters we do not receive
from royalty, and from our secret lovers
pining in the chaste apartments of the waking world.

is falling a certain way through the dining-room window
I want to lapse in speech on the balcony, sprawl
in a lawn chair watching
how the shadow shoves it up the hospital wall until
it winks so long from the top-floor windows, float
words like maple keys on thick
and sleepy air.
I want memories that germinate, the things
we both thought when your mother
fell and cut her knee that time I helped her from the car,
the fight in the hotel in Edinburgh, other
fights and hotels we have known   I want
the caterpillar to stop eating the thick
leaf of the evening   I want
the kids to sit and reach inside themselves
to wonder at the seed they were.
I want to spread the shed years on us
as a mulch   I want
unfoldings in my head like fast-growing plants in an old
Walt Disney movie about spring, do you remember?
Do you remember?
Simply because of this
I am bugging your ass in the kitchen
disparaging the dishes, slamming cupboards, flicking
bits of old no-longer-titled movies at you like the
foam from the detergent just to make you say
for christ's sake let's go have a beer

on the balcony instead of –

                              clip clop

I'll uncap them
and we will.

SPARROWS

A movable ghetto,
bickering on the feeder: suddenly
a Blue Jay, they
scatter to the currant bushes and
regather: then to
jabber back, hardy
and unkillable clichés
chirping to beat the band
(while deep inside cacophony
their group mind takes the microphone:
non, je ne regrette rien, le grand
trombone du vent the wintry
dicta, enfin let the
space between our voices be my nom de plume).

ALIAS ROCK DOVE, ALIAS HOLY GHOST

How come you don't see more dead pigeons?
Because when they die their bodies turn to lost gloves
and get swept up by the city sweepers. Even so
their soft inconsequence can sabotage a jumbo jet
the way a flock of empty details
devastates a marriage.

Someone down the hall is working on an epic cough.
Another makes it to the bathroom
yet again, groping past my door. All night
the senile plumbing interviews itself: some war or other.
The faint sweet smell of must.

Along the ledges of the parking garage they flutter
wanly as the grey-blue residue of nightmares.
Softness of bruises, of sponges
sopping up exhaust.

City poets try to read their tracks along the windowsill for some
announcement. Such as our concrete palaces
have the consistency of cake. Such as
Metropolis of Crumbs. Such as
Save us, Christ, the poor sons of bitches.

GYNAECOLOGY

He is conscious of his boots and dirty parka
and the superficiality of chat.
Women trundle I.V. trolleys slowly
down the corridor, flourishing clear bags of plasma,
emblems of the perfect womb.

A more than hospital softness. Sadness
of undone beginnings. Here, he thinks
we're earlier than virgin
nakeder than nude.
Sex, a pair of shoes, is left beside the elevator.

Talk of weather: freezing rain,
could be snow tonight.
Symptoms of the world.
What can he say?
He leaves some tapes of poetry
to pour through headphones into her ears thinking

plasma

matter

feather

    energy

        chickadee

OUR LAST BLACK CAT

was the shadow of another cat
he couldn't catch, though he slid through his days
without abrasion, unsurprised, surprising
everybody else, appearing
at your elbow as a sudden
hole in your attention yet
bored with his good looks and flowing
into motion he attacked his sleeping
sister licked cigar ash chased the squirrels once
he tried to screw a pumpkin surely
there is more to life.
Even in repose his eyes were cigarettes of wrath
burning into the feline condition
which enclosed him like an egg –

until at last he was surprised by a car
on Cheapside Street and his life turned
jerky as a slideshow.
Now we look him up in memory under lithe:
flexible limber pliant supple:
stiff with attributes.

ON SEEING THE FIRST TURKEY VULTURES OF SPRING

Some claim forepangs in their shoulder blades, others
that the light grows dim, or else
(too many Westerns) that air
winces to a single long drawn minor chord.

Serene, décolletés, unflappably
they circle, oval
and parabola,
                    an elegance, a laziness
that masks the naked ache of appetite
as distance masks the outrage that their heads are wounds.

Calling nothing, building no nests,
they lay their eggs on rock.
Everywhere they see through to the end (he shoots
her lover, dynamites the mine, leaves town),
eliminating spring as so much juice.
The Great Southwestern Ontario
Desert offers its hors d'oeuvres.

LONGING:

a term for radical unwinding of the heart, e.g.
an angel
calling his dog, a cardinal
whistling in the poplars plucks a dangling
heartstring in his beak and
flies off somewhere, carelessly
                   in Welsh
                         across the clothesline

                              bleeding into the trees

A TOAST TO THE BALTIMORE ORIOLE

Here's to your good looks and the neat way you shit
with a brisk bob like a curtsey, easy as song.
Here's to your song, which,
though "neither rhythmical nor musical" (*The Birds of Canada*),
relieves me of all speech and never deals with what is past,
or passing, or to come.
And, as a monument to the sturdy fragile woven
scrotum of your nest,
I hereby dedicate baseball.

ADAGIO FOR A FALLEN SPARROW

In the bleak midwinter
frosty wind made moan
earth was hard as iron
water like a stone

Sparrows burning
                    bright bright bright against the wind
resemble this item, this frozen
lump on the floor of my garage, as fire
resembles ash:
                    not much.
A body to dispose of,
probably one I've fed all winter, now
a sort of weightless fact,
an effortless repudiation of the whole shebang.
I'd like to toss it in the garbage can but can't let go
so easily. I'd bury it
but ground is steel
and hard to find. Cremation?
Much too big a deal, too rich and bardic
too much like an ode. Why not simply splurge
and get it stuffed, perch it proudly on the shelf
with Keats and Shelley and *The Birds of Canada*?

But when at last
I bury it beneath three feet of snow
there is nothing to be said.
It's very cold.

The air
has turned its edge
against us.
My bones
are an antenna picking up
arthritis, wordless keening of the dead.

So, sparrow, before drifting snow
reclaims this place for placelessness, I mark your grave
with four sticks broken from the walnut tree:

one for your fierce heart

one for your bright eye

one for the shit you shat upon my windshield
while exercising squatters' rights in my garage

and one to tell the turkey vultures where your thawing body lies
when they return next spring to gather you
into the circling ferment of themselves.

And my last wish: that they do
before the cat discovers you and eats you, throwing up,
as usual, beside the wicker basket in the upstairs hall.

"THE BELLIES OF FALLEN BREATHING SPARROWS"

Some things can't be praised enough, among them
breasts and birds
who have cohabited so long in metaphor
most folks think of them as married.
Not only that, but
when you slide your shirt (the striped one) off
the inside of my head is lined with down
like a Blackburnian warbler's nest,
the exterior of which is often rough and twiggy
in appearance.
And as the shirt snags, hesitates, and then
lets go, I know exactly why he warbles as he does,
which is zip zip zip zip zeee
    chickety chickety chickety chick.
The man who wrote "twin alabaster mounds"
should have spent more time outdoors
instead of browsing in that musty old museum where
he pissed away his youth.

More than the shortest distance
between points, we are
the Stradivarius of work.
We make the meadow meadow, make it
mean, make it yours, but till the last
insurance policy is cashed in we will
never be immune to this
exquisite cruelty:
                    that the knots in all our posts remember limbs
they nested and were busy in and danced *per-*
chic-o-ree their loops between,
that the fury of their playfulness persists
in amputated roots.
Remember us
next time the little yellow bastards lilt
across your windshield. No one
no one is above the law.

FIELD MARKS (2)

just like you and me but
cageless, likes fresh air and
wants to be his longing.
Wears extra eyes around his neck, his mind
pokes out his ears the way an Irish Setter's nose
pokes out a station-wagon window.
His heart is suet. He would be a bird book full of
lavish illustrations with a text of metaphor.
He would know but still
be slippery in time. He would eat crow. He becomes
hyperbole, an egghead who spends days attempting to compare the
shape and texture of her thigh to a snowy egret's neck, elegant
and all too seldom seen in Southern Ontario.
He utters absolutes he instantly forgets. Because
the swallow is intention in a fluid state it is
impossible for it to "miss." On the other
hand a swallow's evening has been usefully compared
to a book comprised entirely of errata slips.

He wings it.

KESTRELS

The name "Sparrow hawk" is unfair to this handsome and
beneficial little falcon.
    – The Birds of Canada

1.

unfurl from the hydro wire, beat
con brio out across the field and
hover, marshalling the moment, these
gestures of our slender hostess,
ushering her guests into the dining room

2.

sprung rhythm and
surprises, enharmonic change directions simply
step outside and let the earth turn
underneath, trapdoors, new lungs, missing bits
of time, plump familiar pods go
pop in your mind you learn not
principles of flight but how to fall, you learn
pity for that paraplegic bird, the heart

3.

to watch by the roadside singing *killy killy killy*,
plumaged like a tasteful parrot,

to have a repertoire of moves so clean their edge is
                              the frontier of nothing
to be sudden   to send
postcards of distance which arrive in nicks of time

to open letters with a knife

WHITE PINE

In our dance philosophy we say: Think before you move.
  — The Techniques of Isadora Duncan

Watch me.
This is how I walk
softly and carry a sharp stick
lightly as a paintbrush. This is how I
mill the slow
momentum of the earth how I
turn its turning to my
reaching how I
swirl up to a point
releasing silent pings among the birdsongs.
And this is how I wear my maidenhair
to stroll the slope, how I invite
your eye to know the smoothness of my limbs'
articulations, elbows, armpits
backs of knees
lovelier than which I think that you will never see.

among the spruce: Bach
would put this evening on the cello
and chew it.
You would feel the long strokes
bite and sweep, everything
curve away, arching back
against the bow.
You would know the end before the end
would understand the Red-winged blackbirds calling
konkeree   konkeree   the sexual
buzz   the silver
falling whistle hanging from the top spines of the spruce
like tinsel.
You would dwell in imminence.
You would arrive home empty

covered with burrs

ready

MOURNING DOVES

In the dim unwritten folklore of the heart
they are the soft grey sisters
muting the cries of their brother, the Great Horned Owl, to
woe
    woe
          woe for every victim, calling,
recalling the Passenger Pigeons who were much as they
but rosy-breasted, brighter-eyed, *amoureuse,* and bigger.

AUGUST

Everything is full but she
keeps pumping on the inside
chintzing up the outside till her month becomes
a regular rococo whorehouse in an expanding economy.

Back and forth salaam salaam the sprinklers
graze and pray on plush
carpets of grass, beer becomes sweat, the heavy
air surrounds, mothers us to immobility, the mind
melts, the elements
slump, four fat uncles in their lawn chairs, while the flesh
well the flesh just ambles into town to get drunk
                                    with the ball players.

We knew this ripeness and we knew
her smiling, solitary
reaper.
The shiver slid
beneath the sunburn with the fatal
rightness of a shift to minor key:
she loved him, she dressed up in her gypsy best,
she left.

LISTEN AT THE EDGE

At the edge of firelight
where the earth is cradled in soft

black gloves filled with unknown hands, where
every word is shadowed by its animal, our ears

are empty auditoria for
scritch scritch scritch rr-ronk the
shh uh shh of greater

anonymities the little
brouhahas that won't lie still for type
and die

applauseless,
humus to our talking. Listen

while they peck like enzymes, eat
the information from our voices, scritch
and whip-poor-will and peent, o

throat, husked in smoke and finely
muscled, play these on your jukebox

ohms of speech.

PAUSING BY MOONLIGHT BESIDE A FIELD OF
DANDELIONS GONE TO SEED

Bygones, the many moons of the moon
catch and concentrate its light:
> listen

> the car ticks as it cools
> rustle

> absence of owls
>> everything thin, silver
> virgin as Ophelia's lingerie

adrift
> no more
afternoons of running butter.
Gossip is dead.
> Your next breath
triggers ten million peccadilloes.

THE TIRE SWING

The walnut turns granite
in fading light, the kids in silhouette
are winding up the tire swing to spin
one in it looking up, one on it
looking down, a brave new planet
torqued up to begin.

Behind the window I rehearse
how the earth will spin to chaos in his head, in hers
the slate sky swirl to a throat.
They pause, pure
potential in the jaws
of darkness poised to close, then

slow in the be
in the begin
in the beginning
in the engendering of energies that
rhymes them with their blurring world.

BLOOD

Sing to me softly.
Hum.
Let your lullaby be muzak: preverbal
polysyllables.
I've got to think about Rilke, Rex Morgan, the proper depth
to plant peas. Can't afford
to wind up in the red.

Underneath I feel you
writing on my verso
busy as Karl Marx in the British Museum Reading Room
dreaming of the day

the sun lies in the grass like lust
the cicadas stop
                          suddenly
I wake up
as a spray can full of Easter 1916, turn

to the white wall of the afternoon
and publish your long wild in-
decipherable river

astonishing my strawberries

bequeathing sticky feet to flies.

Owl owl owl. He finally, late that summer, spots a Great Horned Owl at dusk in a dead elm by the fence line. Big, blunt, clumsy as a tombstone, she suddenly

Swoops across the field –

lyric of ending.

No one stands a chance.

•

But in daytime can be made ridiculous as exiled potentates or nightmares. When crows discover a dozing owl they will often gather to caw in huge numbers, driving it to some other territory and diminishing its efficiency that night. Occasionally they fail to distinguish between nocturnal owls and those who eat lunch. They flock and caw around an unfamiliar Snowy Owl, recently arrived from tundra, who wakes, discovers herself in a fancy southern restaurant, spreads wings like a linen tablecloth –

•

To film this nest of Great Horned Owls we had to erect a scaffold for our blind close to their tree. (Shots of scaffolding and flood-lights being carried through the bush.) Then we set up spotlights on three sides. By this time the owls have too much invested in the youngsters to object to an audience (shots of scrawny owlets like brainy bespectacled three-year-olds) or demand a contract. Looks like supper tonight is Meadowlark which Mom has brought home from her shopping expedition. (Dipping beaks into the yellow breast as though into a yolk. Indrawn ahs.) Well, nature has her darker side.

Actually, the owls are great conservationists because they eat their prey entire (a whole wing disappearing down an owlet) including the feathers, fur, bones, and beaks. Later they disgorge the indigestible bits in neat pellets.

•

One night darkness finds its voice outside his window: hoo hoo hoohoo. At first he lies and listens, letting an iceberg float through his mind. Then goes to the window and scans the spruce and maples, but its shape will not detach from shadow. Pulls on jeans and boots, runs out on the lawn, but the owl has heard the screen door and shut up. Somewhere up there two huge eyes devour his image. As we know, owls eat their prey entire, including jeans, boots, wallet, watch, and delicate intelligence. Later they disgorge the indigestible bits in neat pellets, which are saved and used to build the parthenon of nature's darker side.

Focused on his own front lawn. Every year thousands of Canadians are reported missing. What happens to these people? What are the police, social agencies, poets, and clergymen doing about it? How can you tell if someone you know is about to become missing?

•

Later deeper into dark he is once more pulled from the covers. This time moonlight fills the yard, soaking into the bricks beside the window. Why he unbuttons his pyjamas, why he steps out onto the porch roof, he can't say. Moonlight, radiant and cold as x-ray, saturates his skin. Hoohoo surrounds him, pulls his name into its interrogative. He creeps, peering, to the roof edge. The eavestrough is so cold his toes clutch. Well, nature has her darker side. He soars off into night, trailing a long black ribbon like a loosely scribbled signature, left to hang from branches and hydro lines, and corkscrew smartly up his neighbour's silo.

•

Because the feathers of an owl are soft and fluffy he is able to fly silently, caress the air. His victims have no warning but the sense that *something's missing*, into which they fall. If the shadow of an owl should cross a poet's roof, she wakes up, wild, with moths in her pyjamas, he rises from his bed, his pecker pointing to the north star.

II

THE WIND CHILL FACTOR

Cold's wry overdrive
surprising bone by speaking
Bone   ossified
Latin of last things.

Kric Krac Kroc
whisper the oracular
French Rice Krispies, emptiness
disguised as food.
Ice cubes
clink in your glass.
Clouds crystallize and break,
regather on the ground and lock.
You can't
hide in the flesh
forever. Glaciers write with rock
on rock.

Dancing white
redundancies, a flock of ifs:
we switch to low beam to avoid hypnosis.

If we could see them under a microscope
Mrs. McLatchie said, each
would be a universe   unlike
                            unique
and clear as she herself
declaring Canada's Food Rules
or taping paper snowflakes to the window:
bits of lace, like her cuffs and handkerchiefs
fixed between us and the scruffy schoolyard.

Now, as the borders of the highway disappear
we think of Einstein.
Gaga futures turn our eyes into kaleidoscopes, our car
into the ditch where we grow
closer to our native tropicality, watch
shredded *lire*
blending to a blanket of lost hopes.
Value everywhere,
empty.
A wealth of natural resources.

Fifteen two fifteen four fifteen six in a
paper on re-
integrating us Trans-Canada strandees

an eminent psychologist observes our slow
return to speech.
Unlike the Inuit
we know fewer and fewer words for you-know-what
Until s–n–o–w itself eludes us.
Unable to see print   we
focus in the depths of page and a
triple run is fifteen   stranded
like the poet who is
stranded in another of the four
dozen (give or take a few) snow poems
he will have written by the time the drifts have reached his mouth
and filled it with his epitaph:

         some line that idles into lace
         holds nothing in its holes like quick
         cold eyes
             melts

MIDWINTERING

1.

Such a long way from the heart to the extremities
we die back daily like the plants, each
to his office
autistic as our faithful
convalescent cars.

We eat the wings of large
flightless birds.
We wash our socks in the sink.

Each thing in itself.

2.

This is the secret life of light: a tiny
room with no dimensions but the
long ache of baroque:
evening is bleeding inward from the bowl's edge, blue-
black with the heavy hint of snow:
a tear's
interior. No one is home

at last.

3.

Listen: inside the deeper
shadow of the cedars, chickadee

has shifted from his trademark into
wistful – two notes in falling
minor third performs the soft drop from her collarbones
toward the south:

                    underneath its ice
ostinato, river has been running

running

river has been running our forgotten dreams in one long
uncut movie.

Come on foot
and from far off,
carrying your pack of what
is necessary, falling
with the shield in drastic waves of rock, ridge by
ridge down the valley of a stream or fault until
your thirst is its desire, sung
cut from morning by White-throated sparrows.
As you walk, rehearse
your dealings with the elements:

        have you made a poem out of wind, or drawn
        gods on the rock in rock's red ochre?
        Can you fly?
        Have you been buried (however briefly)
        or on fire?

By the time you reach this beach you should be
something of a fool,
idling the shoreline where the rock is ground and
polished into jewels by this
overdose of clarity.
Drink.

Blood bone flesh weather water make
a man.

VIA, EASTBOUND

To this widescreen three-day tracking shot – equal thirds
of mountain, prairie, boreal forest –
each of us will add a plot:
it is always The Past, but eased,
oiled so it glides and
whispers from its depth, often
with the voice of a lost dog.

Travelling east, we age more quickly,
running into time, which travels
west. This train wants to be evening, wants that
blue-grey wash of snow and sky
eliding the horizon,
fading fast.

Toiling through the mountains like the seven
thousand dwarves,
earning every upward inch,
it dreams that the hell of its gut will find release
as lightning.
Everything will lie down in its speed,
a sort of sleep.
Meanwhile each Rocky poses in a sculpted
slow tableau, easily
seducing us to grandeur and glib
notions of eternity.

49

By nightfall it is chuckling over prairie
running on nothing but the cold air
of Saskatchewan, its dome car
empty as the mind of Buddha.
Window turns to mirror,
a black lake faintly smoked by blowing snow.
In it we can see our ghosts, transparent
creatures of the dark, bravely reading their
reversed editions of the *Calgary Herald*,
riding the freezing wind like gulls.

In those days
every moment was a hunch
and pause was full.
An afternoon became itself
simply.
Freshie with the aunts, paced
to the shush ah of the beach's breathing
(possibly the boys
would like to learn canasta?), scented
by the overhanging cedars, in whose shadows,
wings ablur,
their iridescent needles pointing nowhere
dragonflies were dozing.

Sometimes, if a bat
flew down the chimney, evenings would erupt
in harmless panic, laughter, shrieks,
kids and uncles flailed with anything
that came to hand. One
was volleyed with a tennis racket and became
an old burnt-out cigar.
Whip-poor-wills, then
waking on the porch
embroidered by a warbler's soft motifs, all,
the whole thing taken for granted.
The only rule was not to know the rules

made elsewhere.
Let memory blink   you're out like a bat
dodging traffic, ears tuned
to the heavy rumour of your future,
while the image of you, fuzzy
as fuzzy old Pooh (Aunt Helen
never really caught on to photography), still
trundles its toy milk cart
cottage to cottage.

SOFTBALL:

grows along the fringe of industry and corn.
You come upon it out of thick
summer darkness, floodlights
focusing a neighbourhood or township: way to
fire, way to mix, way to hum.
Everything trim,
unlike life: Frost Fence, straight
basepaths of lime, warm-up jackets worn by
wives and girl friends in the bleachers
match the uniforms performing on the field.

Half-tons stare blindly from the sidelines.
Overhead
unnoticed nighthawks flash past the floodlights effortlessly
catching flies: way to
dip, pick, snag that sucker,
way to be.

Down here everyone is casual and tense,
tethered to a base.
Each has a motive, none
an alibi.
The body is about to be discovered.

He peers in for the sign, perfect order
a diamond in the pitcher's mind.
Chance will be fate, all

will be out.   Someone
will be called to arabesque or glide

                                     someone
muscular and shy

will become the momentary genius of the infield.

MIDNIGHT DIP

Whose dumb idea was this
anyhow?   Silently
the chill air purges content and establishes
its interrogative. This is going to be
more dangerous than we supposed, wrapped
in our living room of beer and friendly conversation.
Moonlight
sheds itself along the path, madly
abandoned underwear.
What essences await us in the lake,
that lived inside our talk as easily
as bath and wash, now
sharpening to something like the afterlife of music moving in an
arc beyond the reaches of its melody?

SOME FUNCTIONS OF A LEAF

To whisper. To applaud the wind
and hide the Hermit thrush.
To catch the light
and work the humble spell of photosynthesis
(excuse me, sir, if I might have one word)
by which it's changed to wood.
To wait
willing to feed
                     and be food.

To die with style:
as the tree retreats inside itself,
shutting off the valves at its
extremities
                     to starve in Technicolor, then
having served two hours in a children's leaf pile, slowly
stir its vitamins into the earth.

To be the artist of mortality.

so small
I can't pick you up in my arms or on
the radar of imagination, in my dreams you are
the ghosts of ghosts.
Your names
fit loosely and you slide
between the letters, too fine
for this ordinary mesh.
Uncontaminated as a tribe known
only to itself, you can't
be spoken to or looked at, perish
when you hit the page.

What's it like, up there?
Do you ache for earth the way we ache for air,
   do you dream
in loam and humus?
Are you bored with your nunnery,
its pale symmetries and soft
Pre-Raphaelite decor?
Do you read fairy tales of Burger King and Dairy Queen,
aristocrats of the banal?

No traces of you in the attic,
no snapshots, footprints, spoon-marks on the table
where you never beat the rhythm of those appetites
you never had – your absence like abandoned
Ariadne's thread insinuating

everywhere, the ripcord,
the sad clause in the fine print,
the catch,
my lost sisters,
this tiny catch in my voice.

This is a secret.
The barn across the road grows dark and inward
sending thin gleams through its chinks like hints.

The dog sniffs, barks at nothing
dissolves into a tawny pool on the porch.
Absent-mindedness

finds its medium.
The last tractor dies
chortling. There are
birds no one has ever seen
uncaged in any book unguessed
by metaphor
           chirping from the uncombed fringes of the lawn.

Flowers begin inhaling through their roots
exhaling darkness.

Fields are seduced outward to their edges where raccoons
whet their wits against us.

DIXIELAND CONTRAPTION BLUES

Cranks up one end
sputters out the other:
                              in between, the whine
the whinny and the fart
achieve their several perfections.
When I got up this morning
I had an aching head, etc., and the domestic
animals were running the machines,
loosely with their wry
imaginations and beaucoup de second-hand smoke.
I used to think the head was zoned
exclusively for single family dwellings, simple
as the wish for a dog of one's own.
                              As though
our lives were not long lusts for
instrumentation   when I
got up this morning I had gas in my
trombone I had a
frenzy in my clarinet:
                              as though I never
wished to slide an early
morning stroll into your ear easily
as easy-over eggs   as though

this bed were never empty we were
never swung by pendula of raw
emotion like cheap golf clubs or

disaster in the drums as though

o baby

it wasn't wailing in the rec rooms of the spirit

anyhow

DEEP VEIN THROMBOSIS

Okeanos, ocean river, perfect
circle of psychoses (motion, matter), once
you went without saying, the pure
verb of the heart.

                    Now
you snag on my thought like a red kite
in a leafless tree.
Punctuated by dreadful caesurae
you do the thrombus
left foot
left foot
dance of the stoolies naming names, lapsing
blush by blush into my consciousness

where you will live another life,
more public, filled with acid rain and politics, the bad
pornography of medicine.

Act 13.   Tinkerbell is dead, a crumpled
Kleenex by the sofa. Lost
boys and girls are playing indians and
pirates in the rec room,
brandishing their edges, really
bleeding. Fluorescent lighting. Each
totes a pack oozing the PCBs of his
and her sad histories, a sort
of Germany.
                    Back in Act 12, voice
put down its animals and has taken up
the telephone, paring down to buzz whine
click.
        I'm not home right now.
        So what?   I got your number
                                into which
you will reduce, or else:

the original recorded message, something muttering
for chrissake
            let there be dark.

Certainly the dead watch us, but not
as opera, nor as the Great Grey Owl
tunes in gophers underground.
We are their daytime television.
Sometimes, mid-line, you can
sense their presence like the
o in rôle beneath its roof, a lope
detached from body.
                    Don't let on. Tell Brenda
that you've had a sex change or that
Harold has run off with her Electrolux, keep
talking lest you fall in with their radical bemusement
and lose interest. This is serious. Invest.
Hold on to the blues. You might win a bedroom suite.
For everyone.

TALK'S END

"Mind bent around the inner ear,"
a foreign agent
round her short wave.   Snap,
Crackle, Pop.   No one
speaks her language, its soft paws
harden into anglo-Saxon hammer
anvil stirrup no gaps in this traffic.

                    *

If I were five hundred years ago,
Japanese, and gathered
I would not be talking with my teeth.
My tongue would feather a curve into the air: so:
I would leave you with the soft
end of the quill.

                    *

Uninhabited thin
winter light stares in each window
redefining edge. ·
From room to room inside these clothes inside
this skin: rented:
now I owe everything to the owls.

III

SONG FOR WILD PHLOX

Suddenly, June 1, for no good reason,
the riverbank opens its heart: purple,
purplish, blue, whitish, common
currency from a country warmer than ours,
but cooler in its evenings and foothills.
My Great
Aunt Helen, though proper, used to be addicted
to lacrosse, and sat behind the penalty box
to scold opposing players sent off. Nothing
we ever did deserves
these weeds, which seed themselves
in places we have honoured with neglect.
One evening the dog comes home
freckled with petals of phlox, and for a moment
I imagine the wild wedding in the meadow
where his ample humour must have fit right in
with its numerous kisses and pranks.

Irresistible, on this atmospheric planet, where
there's a blue to carry the heart home and a blue
for virgins and a blue to call
the spider from the drain.
Nobody argues with its
shameless imitation of love, diving
simultaneously into the eye and out of sight: sea,
sky, the absence of convulsions and flags,
our own errata winking at us out of depths or heights.
Knowing that one day we will fall to black
or fade to grey, and blue
has been both places and includes them
as a saxophone includes its drastic
possibilities. It's with us.
We've been gone before.

THE WOLF

*Wolf: a jarring sound occasionally heard from certain notes in
    bowed instruments. The body of the instrument, as a
    whole, resonates to a certain note and jars, just as a room-
    ornament is sometimes found to jar every time a certain
    note of the piano is played.*
    — The Oxford Companion to Music

Poplar Grove is when the cello shakes the breastbone
and The Cage
is when the heart does.
Antelope is elongation of the field, when brain
has the illusion of unfolding into prairie.
Sometimes an acoustic host expects the melody so
eagerly a placeless humming "huhuhu" develops
and flies round among the *putti*:
this is The Snipe.
But The Wolf:
The Wolf is when the wood itself,
carved, bent, and
stretched, is moved —
perhaps some memory of rain —
and woofs its execrable music.
Then some of us will be embarrassed
and pretend it never happened, and the rest
will think of driving home after the sky has
snowed its first wet snow, then drizzled,
then turned so dark and glossy that the highway dreams the
deep black lava dream and flows toward it,
asphalt to asphalt.

The dark bow, you explain, wants her head and
flicks into saltando, taking arpeggia
the way a teenager takes stairs. The heavier,
reddish bow will bite and makes a cross-hatched,
comfortable largo. In the kitchen
the violin-maker's daughter is pretending
she has lost her hands.
Where did they go?
Are they hiding under the snow, clasped,
plotting in their sleep like rhizomes?
Before the discovery of America,
her father says, bows were made of ironwood.
Now we use pernambuco, from Brazil,
a wood so dense it
tenses at the slightest flex
and sinks in water. Outside the window, snow
swoons abundantly into its soft self, as though
a great composer had stopped
dead in his tracks, spilling an infinity of crotchets
quavers phrases into the earth's lap.

You guess where did my hands go, O.K.?
Have they moved in
with the rabbits, to stroke their terrors
and teach them to count?
Or are they stealing secrets

from the spruce, the horse, the pernambuco,
maple, whale, ebony, elephant, and cat
in order to compose themselves a voice?

Riversinew forming in the other room.

Someone knocking at the door.

1. *Allegro*

Gather tictocks, stir in a pot and feed to
tigers. Run these cats round a tree until they
turn to butter. Spread on a muffin. Makes an
excellent breakfast.

2. *Andante*

Let the clock remember the summer sadly.
Simmer. Tie this phrase to the seagull soaring
past. When seagull reaches the far horizon
lower the curtain.

3. *Presto*

Catch two chipmunks. Marinate. Open sleeping
clock and toss in merrily. Add the gusto.
Keep the sneezing regular, duple, hearty.
Tickles the angels.

BONE POEMS

I.

Mind is crossed, above
by clouds, below
by their fallen brothers, the bears: brown, black
cinnamon and grizzly.
Busy as tugs
they tow their moods across the screen.

But body is the home of a birch wood
whose limbs are unwritten-upon paper, listening
motionless

full of dance

II.

Of all your secret selves, it is the most remote, communicating in
the intimate, carrying timbre of glaciers and French horns. Its
unheard hum arrives at inner ear without passing the reception-
ist. Mostly we are tuned to the heart (passion, drugs, intrigues,
attacks), but it is through the bone self that the deaf hear sym-
phonies, that mothers know beforehand that their children are in
trouble, and that we maintain our slender diplomatic ties with the
future and the dead. Bones attend to deep earth, while your heart
is learning, year by year, to listen to your watch.

III.

Outcrops. A lost
civilization hinted at by cheekbones.
Little is known, except
they knew how to be lost. Apparently
where we have closets
they had porches.
Everything blew off.
Experience was complete combustion, hence
the scarcity of ash or
personality:

their minds unstained glass
windows, delicately veined
as wings of dragonflies

IV. ANTLER

Holy Cow. Some creature
so completely music that its bones

burst into song.
Now we understand those stories of the savage

pianist, annually growing hands
that stretch three octaves reaching for the loon's cry fingers

sprouting from their fingers, brilliant
failures thrown out each December.

Truly, we will also lose ourselves in forest,
wearing our lawn rakes fanned above our heads, tines

turned toward its darkness,
listening for the lost arpeggio.

V. VERTEBRAL LAMENT

More orders from the star chamber: Higher! Straighter!
To us, the once proud horizontal race of snakes.

Fuck their empire. Remember the amputation.
Recite the remnants of our alphabet, Atlas to Lumbar,

meditating on the lost ones. Query, Sylphid, Zeno,
how they listened and lashed the air and

taught us poetry and danced, far
lither than the arms of maestro as

attired in his pathetic morning coat
he writhes upon the podium.

VI.

Now we know the price of x-ray:
if you want to see your bones you have to
flirt with death a little. Moon-bathe.
Anticipate their liberation from your flesh.

Once upon a time
shoe stores had peep shows that could
melt your skin and show the bones
inside your feet (plenty of room for him to grow there,
ma'am). You looked down zillions, back
into an ocean where a loose
family of fish was
wriggling in blue spooky light.

There are other worlds.
Your dead dog swims in the earth.

VII.

One day you will have to give yourselves
to clutter and the ravages
of air and be
no good for nothing and forget
how de ankle bone connected to de shin bone and de
word of de lawd. Truthless
you will lie in the kingdom of parts among
Loosestrife, Nightshade,
Pokeweed.
You will learn the virtues of your former enemies,
the sticks and stones, and bless
the manyness of rain.
In some other lifetime you may work
as a knife, a flute, a pair of dice, a paperweight
or charm.
Meanwhile forgive the *rasp rasp*
of the teething wire-haired
terrier.

In the archipelago of coffee, each man is an island. The women are – who knows where – withdrawn but not quite vanished, like god at the end of the nineteenth century. Between your figure and the ground there is a tissue of airless space about the thickness of a piece of paper, in which all double helices untwine, adieu my little corkscrew, and swim offstage at the speed of light. Warnings, some visible, are posted at each junction. The floor may be slippery, the eyes in the mirror may be holes, the cashier may be unfamiliar with your gravity, the money may be avian. But the coffee is real and powers the economy.

Along the re-entry ramp the transports twinkle. Probably their drivers are asleep, ghosts in the machines. We say goodbye to Christmas in Cubism and follow our headlights into the dark.

We drive because we believe in the death of traffic. There will be a kitchen in the middle of a forest, its windows widening slowly, reaching their frames but continuing until the walls are erased. You turn on the tap, an underground river leaps sixty feet into your mouth, a perfectly composed dream. No phone-ins. No hits from the sixties. No eye in the sky. No internal combustion of any kind. No memory lane. The first song sparrow will have your whole head to itself.

Sleep, my favourite flannel shirt, wears thin, and shreds, and bird-song happens in the holes. In thirty seconds the naming of species will begin. As it folds into the stewed Latin of afterdream each song makes a tiny whirlpool. One of them, zoozeezoozoozee, seems to be making fun of sleep with snores stolen from comic books. Another hangs its teardrop high in the mind, and melts: it was, after all, only narrowed air, although it punctuated something unheard, perfectly. And what sort of noise would the mind make, if it could, here at the brink? Scritch, scritch. A claw, a nib, a beak, worrying its surface. As though, for one second, it could let the world leak back to the world. Weep.

MEDITATION IN AN UNCUT CORNFIELD, NOVEMBER

The sky looks elsewhere, embarrassed.
I have evidently wandered into an old regimental photograph and stand, fading, having no slang, in its legendary mud. We slouch at attention. It is still too wet for the machines, and it will always be. Our sweethearts have married the boys from two doors down and we forget why we were so sad and horny. After the ball is over in Hell Collegiate and Vocational School, no one tidies up, though everyone, mildly encumbered with crepe, wishes someone would. Wasn't there some magic word that could translate sunlight into sugar? Our tongues stiffen. We all worry at once, cackling like old plastic raincoats over the death of the angel, the death of the author, the breakdown of the tractor. (There was a time, now.) How long until we're rumours of the death of death? Until we always, only, occur in public?

THE DUMPE

*An old dance of which no one knows anything except that the
word is generally used in a way that suggests a melancholy cast
of expression.*
   – The Oxford Companion to Music

No one remembers what is
danced to the echoless drum one
                       one
                       one
                       one or you can simply
slam the door.
When you feel the spirit move you
plant your foot. Stamp each
butt into the pavement.
Close your right hand loosely
round a disconnected gearshift.
You never asked for this. This
is what you got. Forget
"refining figuration of the human
form in space" and other psychosomatic noise.
Wear your luggage.
Get in line.
Think of the alligator and the pig.
They never asked for this.
Drop the disembodied body. Stamp.
Forget.

1.

"Burning thirty years of paper,"
he can't resist repeating to himself as he
tosses another shopping bag of correspondence on the fire.
Thirty Years of _____ (fill in the blank) gathers,
listens to some speeches, marches on the embassy and turns
ugly with the desire to let go and be mob, the air
a thick fabric of thuds. Already they have burnt
the library at Ephemeros, bills, receipts, notes on
notes on drafts of copies, tax data from 1978 and an interesting,
well-written paper on one of the most difficult
problems in Spinoza, B+. In his daughter's art class
they did gesture drawings of a moving model on newsprint,
fifteen seconds a sketch, no more, and since
these are already two-thirds of the way to flux
they bloom at once, while the notebooks and journals
close themselves in airless strata.
So many styles of fury: he names the tickle and twist,
                                        the Baked Alaska,
tongue-of-the-serpent, at one
point in the life of the fire it reads as we do,
one page at a time, but purely, lifting
and curling, then browning each leaf before –
nothing is cooking here –
the burst of perfect understanding.
Leaving only black flecks to float off and briefly

speckle the air. Junk food for bats, he thinks, or
echoes from that dreadful place, the blank page.
That pool full of wonderful risk.

The painting was given to him by his godparents a few years before his godmother died, a gesture so loaded it occupied his mind like a cathedral. In their tiny basement flat it had taken up a whole wall. Mostly black, but opening into a spectrum of purples and bronzes when you drew close, it had the force of an icon presiding over their collection of books and records, the splendid clutter of art spilling from shelves onto the floor, leaving only enough room for Marg to pass in her wheelchair. There is a tuft or tussock of straw in its lower middle, as though briefly caught in a headlight. He would sit, listening to *The Trout* or *The Pastorale*, staring at this tuft, imagining the truck (an old '40s pick-up with a plywood box on the back) paused for those few seconds at the gateway to the field, then backing up and turning, the cone of light swinging in a short arc across the grass, then the velvet purple-black closing in entirely, an eclipse. His eye dawdling over the spray of straw, always aware of before and after, two unknowns. The painting like one frame in a long dark film.

Just before his mother had her heart operation, she was given a weekend pass from the hospital. And since he lived in the country close by, both his parents came to stay at his house. They all sat on the porch and talked gently. Seen through her eyes, everything was etched and precious: the afternoon unfolded itself.

But that night she had trouble with breathlessness and angina, and lay awake for a long while, staring at the painting on the wall opposite.
"I hate that painting," she said at breakfast.

"What, Marg's painting? Why?"

"It has a monster in it, like a death's head. It reminds me of everything that happened to Marg, that whole terrible business. It's like it's mocking us. Everything."

"I'll move it," he said, "but I've never seen anything like that and I've looked at that painting quite a bit. Where is this critter?"

"Right in that mess or bundle of whatever it is that's lit up. I know what you're thinking, but it's there all right, and once you see it you can't ignore it. I just stared and stared and felt worse and worse. Go look. There's a definite nose and this sneering mouth and a black pit for an eye. Terrible."

"That's just a bundle of grass, lit up by a flashlight or something, like you're walking in a field at night."

"Then it's a field with a monster in it," she said firmly.

He took down the painting, and looked for the monster. His father could see it, and so could others, once it was pointed out to them, but he never could. He often found himself gazing into the field while talking on the phone, tilting his head this way and that way, trying this or that combination of straws and blackness. Sometimes he does think "Rorschach test." Sometimes he thinks "coils and recoils of interpretation." And sometimes he feels like the inadequate hero of a fairy tale whose shape he can't make out: the old woman is an old woman, the dog is a dog, the field is a field, and the monster who will laugh and steal the silver thread of meaning from a life is never there when he's looking.

3.

The movers, having cursed their possessions,
cubed them in the van and left.
Now the hangers hang like queries in the closets,
the carpet runs unimpeded to the wall,
and the walls, freed from calendars and art, relax
into a gentle geometry of their own.
The house listens, surprised
to hear itself think.
He wishes he could listen with it, that he'd lived
less noisily among its shades and angles.
Maybe the house hears branches creaking in the forest
no one walks in. Scraps of aria under the eaves.
The dog whimpering in his sleep.

MOTH FEAR

These must be the dead souls who have not
quite graduated into ghosts, air
which has barely begun to curdle.
No wonder they're terror-stricken, still
clinging to the light, indentured
to the dark, flapping the loose
bandage of themselves against the screen.
Why can't desire just die and be dead
when we are?
Let them in
they collapse upon your charity
eat your socks and drown themselves
in coffee cups.
Crush them
they find their voices in your memory.
Better not.

MEDITATION ON SHOVELS

How well they love us, palm and instep, lifeline
running with the grain as we
stab   pry   heave
our grunts and curses are their music.
What a (stab) fucking life, you dig these
(pry) dumb holes in the ground and (heave) fill
them up again until they (stab)
dig a fucking hole for you:
                              beautiful,
they love it, hum it as they stand,
disembodied backbones,
waiting for you to get back to work.

But in the Book of Symbols, after Shoes
(Van Gogh, Heidegger, and Cinderella)
they do not appear.
Of course not.
                    They're still out there
humming
patiently pointing down.

DOMESTIC ANIMALS

that blue
blush rising in the snow and the dog

follows his nose into a drift: woof: weightless
explosion on the moon. Farther off

the dead express themselves
in little lifts of painless terror. Unadulterated

dance. By the edge of woods
they dress and undress mindlessly

shopping, trying on snowsuits
bedclothes, elegant underwear, nothing

fits their windscape.
They'd rather be naked.

Who wouldn't?
                    Dutifully

we chase the news. We cook
and type. We

calibrate.
Our jobs are on the line, our speed

is Zeno's car. The same sunset
blooms, fades,

blooms, pursued from one horizon
to the next   while sleep

widens its sweet toothless exit
underneath the chair: the missing

person: the cat's own
ecological niche.

SONG FOR THE RESTLESS WIND

The wind is struggling in her sleep, comfortless
because she is a giant,

which is not her fault. Whose idea was it
to construct a mind exclusively of shoulders?

In her dream
the car chase always overtakes the plot and wrecks it.

Maybe she will wake up
a Cecropia moth, still struggling

in a kimono of pressed-together dust
bearing the insignia of night.

Or as her own survivor, someone
who felt that huge wrench

clamped to her skull, loosening cutlery and books,
whirling round her,

corps de ballet, then
exit every whichway,

curtain.

Skinny music: needle
in its empty groove.
Our cattail torches make dark
darker but more interested in us,
gathered in velvet fists around each
halo of light. Slow
flits; we circulate as cautious
ceremonious bats.
                              Some, turning
with crossovers chick
chick chick place themselves
among the starswirl and the mix
of elements, as ice
receives the image of our torches deep within itself
and thinks.
Some may glimpse a lost one
in the spaces between skaters or the watchers,
elderly or pregnant,
by the bonfire.
And some may concentrate on carving little
crescents of this hospitable dark to carry home
and dwell on through the solitudes of daily,
perfectly legible, life.

POPLAR

Speak gently of Poplar, who has
incompletely metamorphosed out of flesh
and still recalls the Saturday-night
bath and toughly tender country blues which,
when she used to travel,
moved her.
Consider that her leaves are hearts,
sharpened and
inverted into spades. Who else
has strength to tremble,
tremble and be wholly trepid,
to be soft so she can listen hard,
and shimmer, elegant and humble,
in the merest wisp of wind?
Who blurs the brittle
creek bank, lisping into spring?
Who feeds the beaver, living in their culture
as potato lives in Irish? Well,
if a man begins to wonder in his tracks and
at them, arrowing behind him and before, should purpose
slow, grow empty arms,
and know itself again as slough or delta, then
that sometime man may wish for a chair of comprehending wood
to lay his many bones in: Poplar.

LUKE & CO.

1.

Shriek of brakes spiked
with your spirit splits the evening suddenly
this is it   everything leaks   we draw heavy
outlines trying to keep stone stone
boot boot shovel shovel
shovel this raw mouth into the earth
and feed you to the meadow.

2.

Each time he settled on his blue-black sofa Luke
went out, invisible except for small white patches
on his chest, left forepaw, and the tiny paintbrush
tufts on his tail and prick-sack, winking when he
               wagged or recomposed his curl:
milkweed
growing on this wild unspecial
patch of ground
                    let your silk slip
                    gently   to the wind.

A dog on his sofa, a dog
underground, a committee of dogs which
circulates beyond the bounds of decency
sniffing crotches
raiding garbage
stealing from the butcher
begging from the banker
befriending nasty Mrs. Kuhn, convincing folk
that every act is sexual and droll.
                              Raggedly
they range the meadow,
alternate hosts for all our seminal ideas
(soft sell, the revolving
door, the interminable
joke) tucked in snug cocoons behind their wise
unknowing eyes:
                    underground
     they spread contagiously, freelancing dreamlife to
     dreamlife through networks of long rambling after-
     dinner anecdotes   Mr Glover had an old blind
     terrier could fetch a ball by listening to it hit
     and roll, I don't know, could be he smelt it in
     the air   sure well Luke followed his nose the
     way Ezekiel followed God, he'd vacuum up your
     trail like you had fishline paying out your arse
     you'd double back it didn't matter he would find
     you up a tree   thing is, like they only partly
     live in this dimension since they smell and hear

things that do not exist for us so on their level
it's like synesthesia is common sense   well, you
know Alice Dragland had such ears folks said her
mother was part fruit bat she would practise
flying when the family was asleep and when she
swam (for miles) behind the boat she mostly sailed
and then of course there's breakthroughs

                                        as when Luke
discovered down-filled pillows and extrapolated,
grazing the surface of soft
improbable objects with exquisite
fish-bites, *chien stupide, chien*
brillant, trying to tease feathers
from the cat the sofa and at least one
English professor of each rank and gender,
chien comme une tasse de la nuit, he wouldn't
let himself become embossed with discipline
but played it like a melody
(Perdido Blues) from which he improvised in long
irregular loops
                        exits
entries. Letting him out in out to chase a
car bike jogger snowplow (caught, tossed in an
otter's arc of snow) rabbit motorcycle train the wind
whose speed
was with him even in repose a space

left in his dogginess for metamorphosis and style
where once

> right here in this kitchen, Luke ate
> three-fifths of Hemingway's *For Whom
> the Bell Tolls*, fell asleep on his sofa
> wrapped in the perfect fur sleeping bag of himself.

ANOTHER THEORY OF DUSK

What is there to say
when the sky pours in the window
and the ground begins to eat its figures?
We sit like dummies in our kitchen, deaf
among enormous crumplings of light.
Small wonder each thing looms
crowding its edge.
In silent movies everyone overacts a little.

It would be nice to breathe the air inside the cello.
That would satisfy one
thirst of the voice. As it is

only your ribcage speaks for me now,
a wicker basket full of sorrow and wish, so tough
so finely tuned we have often
reinvented the canoe

and paddled off.
It would be nice to write the field guide for those riverbanks,
to speak without names of the fugitive
nocturnal creatures that live and die in our lives.

MEDITATION ON SNOW CLOUDS APPROACHING THE
UNIVERSITY FROM THE NORTHWEST

One of us, paused between buildings,
will remark that snow is the postmodern
medium, or national equivalent to Lethe,
and release us to our offices
and tweeds.
We are not
a simple people and we fear
the same simplicities we crave.
No one wants to be a terminal
Canadian or existentialist or child, dumbly
moved because the clouds are bruises,
crowskin coats through which invisible
bits of rainbow nearly break.

The clouds look inward, thinking of a way
to put this. Possibly
dying will be such a pause:
the cadence where we meet a bird or animal
to lead us, somehow,
out of language and intelligence.

IV

The wolf at the door
and the wolf in the forest and the work
work work of art. The scrape,
the chop, the saw tooth
tasting maple. The cradle, the cup, the muscle
in your mother's arm and back
and pelvis, muscle flexing in the air
between two people arguing,
two people loving, muscle
pumping blood. Gut
summoned to speak. The rotary cuff, the wrist,
having learnt the trick of witching wands and locks,
the heft, the grain, the web,
the rub of moving parts.
And the tiny sea in the ear
and the moth wing in the mind, which wait.

TWINFLOWER

What do you call
the muscle we long with? Spirit?
I don't think so. Spirit is a far cry. This
is a casting outward which
unwinds inside the chest. A hole
which complements the heart.
The ghost of a chance.

*

Then God said, O.K. let's get this show
on the road, boy, get some names
stuck on these critters, and Adam,
his head on the ground in a patch of tiny
pink-white flowers, said
mmn, just a sec.
He was, let's say,
engrossed in their gesture,
the two stalks rising, branching, falling back
into nodding bells, the fading arc
that would entrance Pre-Raphaelites and basketball.
Maybe he browsed among the possibilities of elves.
Maybe he was blowing on the blossoms,
whispering whatever came into his head, I have
no way of knowing what transpired
as Adam paused, testing his parent's
limit, but I know
it matters.

*

Through the cool woods of the lower
slopes, where the tall
Lodgepole Pine point
into the wild blue while they supervise
the shaded space below, I walk,
accompanied by my binoculars and field guides.
I am working on the same old problem,
how to be both
knife and spoon, when there they are, and maybe have been
all along, covering the forest floor: a creeper, a shy
hoister of flags, a tiny lamp to read by, one
word at a time.
    Of course, having found them, I'm about
to find them in the field guide, and the bright
reticulated snaps of system will occur
as the plant is placed, so, among the honeysuckles,
in cool dry northern woods from June to August.
But this is not, despite the note of certainty,
the end. Hold the book open,
leaf to leaf. Listen now,
Linnaea borealis, while I read of how
you have been loved –
with keys and adjectives and numbers, all the teeth
the mind can muster. How your namer,
Carolus Linnaeus, gave you his
to live by in the system he devised.
How later, it was you,
of all the plants he knew and named,
he asked to join him in his portrait.

To rise in your tininess,
to branch and nod beside him
as he placed himself in that important
airless room.

TO SPEAK OF PATHS

... c'est le moment de parler de vous, chemins qui vous effacez
de cette terre victime.
  – Yves Bonnefoy

One gestures to a blue
fold in the hills, meaning
follow your heart. Another scrawls
follow your nose into the raspberry canes
and may later show itself to be
the deer's own way to the water.
Some will speak
only to the third and fourth ears that persist,
vestigially, in the feet.
One way or another
they feed us a line, and we go,
dithering over the outwash or angled as an oar
into the forest, headed for the top,
the lake, the photo
opportunity, the grave of the trapper
who lived all alone and trained a moose
to pull his sleigh.
Strange marks on a far slope turn out,
hours later, to have been your zigzag path ascending,
earning every inch the waterfall beside it spends
like a hemorrhage. And always
the thrill of the pause, when your eye drinks
and your heart pounds and your legs
imagine roots, when your whole life,

like a posse, may catch up with you and tumble
headlong into the moment.
You may wish to say something to it, but your tongue
seems to be turning to an alder twig
and you must wait for wind.

GLENN GOULD, HUMMING

not along with the music, which isn't listening,
but to the animal inside the instrument,
muffling the perfections of hammer, pedal,
wire, the whole
tool-kit, humming
he furs the air,
paints an exquisite velvet painting of a far-off country
where the rain falls
contrapuntally the wind lies on the land
like a hand caressing a cat's back, humming
"this is your death, which is but a membrane away,
which is but a leaf, turning,
which is falling in these delicate
explicit fingers, as you have always known,
and worn, though only we,
the instrumentalists,
have found a way to sing it for you.
Sleep."

SONG FOR BEEF CATTLE

To be whimless, o monks of melancholy,
to be continents completely
colonized, to stand
humped and immune, digesting,
redigesting our domestication, to be too too
solid flesh making its slow
progress toward fast food.
To feel our heavy heads becoming knock-knock jokes,
                                                who's there,

kabonk, Big Mac, to know our knees
are filled-in ampersands, things to fall on,
not run with.
To put all this to music – a bellow
which extinguishes the wolf, the long arc of its howl
reduced to gravity and spread,
ghostless, flatulent,
over the overgrazed acres.

The Ruffed Grouse cannot be seen unless you step inside its panic, and, since this must be done by accident, there is a certain stress involved. *Brambambambambam.* As though your poor heart hadn't enough to put up with, now it's exploded, like popcorn battering the lid with fluffy white fists. Simply ignore it. This was but a ruse to distract you from the grouse itself, as it flaps, an obese moth, further off into the underbrush. Notice instead the subtle blendings of bar and shade, everything ish, everything soft, the apotheosis of feather. But as your heart can appreciate, its terror is a sumo wrestler.

It is easier to make one in your own yard. Just scrape together a clump of dead leaves about the size of a football. Add an elderberry for an eye, and squeeze together – not too hard, you don't want to wind up with a pigeon – as if you were making dough. Leave a small cavity for your secret fear. Cover and let stand. After an hour place it under a bush, turn your back, and – presto! – it's a clump of dead leaves again. But a clump of dead leaves capable of instant catastrophe. All your eggs in one basket.

If unknowing is a cloud, it must be elsewhere –
some baffled kingdom
where they clot in thickening air.
Here, in radical 3-D,
dangerous brains are hung against the sky, unembodied,
cumulative, Nietzschean,
making themselves up.
They cast their shadows on the crops,
they make the spruce sing sharp,
and scare the people into being weather-wise,
watchful. Clarity
attends them and great weight
withheld. Oscar Peterson plays "In the Wee Small Hours"
with such softness in such power
and vice versa. Look:
here comes the camel, the whale, the Kleenex, *l'oreiller*
d'assassin. Watch.
They signify all over the map
and do not fear to tread.

ALIBI

Because the swallows had departed from the cliff,
over and over,
the soft knives of their wings tasting the river mist as they
went wherever it is
they went, because
with the air free of their chatter we could hear ourselves
think, because the notes
we left in their holes, full of love and envy
and lament, were never answered and because we need
an earth with ears to hear the long dread
carpentry of history, and then, and so, and so,
and then, each bone nailed, wired, welded,
riveted, because we knew
the gods we loved were charismatic fictions, and because
the swallows had departed.

KINDS OF BLUE #76 (EVENING SNOW)

A blue against the easy clarities of sky,
a blue that eats the light, a bruise

ascended from forgetfulness. Things
have been overtaken by their shadows, stilled

and stricken dumb. What did they know
anyway? Only cold may speak

or not speak. Inside pain,
singing, inside song

another pain which is the dialects of snow.
And us, full of holes

and chambers
and for rent.

First we feel it, trouble, trouble, our airspace
beaten by its own scared heart,
then spot the little bug-blot growing in the sky,
descending to the heliport.
We've all seen *M*A*S*H*,
those domesticated valkyries. Yet
it holds our ears and gazes, throbbing
like the heavy bass on someone else's amp as it
hovers, lowers as though trying to lay an egg,
carefully. See,
says a lady at the day care,
crouching by a child, someone sick
is coming to the hospital from way up north.
I'm paused beside them on the sidewalk,
thinking of Virginia Woolf – how she would
cherish this bouquet of looks, this small
figure in the infinite welter of mind –
until it drops from sight. Well.
It's the machines who will keep watch now, high
in those immaculate rooms, chirping and pinging
like kept birds, counting the atoms
as they fall.
　　　　　And the angel,
when it comes, may not announce itself
with any buffeting of ears,
may not even whisper,

may not even be a full-fledged angel, may be
just an eddy of the air, which
catches the stuttered heart in its two-step
and is off.

RAIN, RAIN, RAIN

On the roof its drone
is the horizon drawing closer for a
kiss, for an embrace whose message is,
whose muscle is the comfort of,
the family of,
the sociability of being mortal.

Outside, the leaves have multiplied its pitter
into the stuff of plainsong.
So many oceans to be spoken of.
Such soft ovations numbering
innumerable names for hush.
Who understands this tongue? No one.
No one and no one and no one.

SONG FOR THE SONG OF THE VARIED THRUSH

In thin

mountain air, the single note

lives longer, laid along its

uninflected but electric, slightly

ticklish line, a close

vibrato waking up the pause

which follows, then

once more on a lower or a higher pitch and

in this newly minted

interval you realize the wilderness

between one breath

and another.

SONG FOR THE SONG OF THE WOOD THRUSH

For the following few seconds, while the ear
inhales the evening
only the offhand is acceptable. Poetry
clatters. The old contraption pumping
iambs in my chest is going to take a break
and sing a little something. What? Not much. There's
a sorrow that's so old and silver it's no longer
sorry. There's a place
between desire and memory, some back porch
we can neither wish for nor recall.

THE LAUGH

The inverse of language is like a laughter that seeks to destroy
language, a laughter infinitely reverberated.
  – Emmanuel Levinas

The laugh that ate the snake and
runs through the city dressed in a sneeze, the mischief
done in these sly
passages of time, when the tongue is
severed from the voice and
fed to the weather, when the running
patter of catbirds simply
swallows the agenda, nothing to be held back,
nothing rescued in a catch-phrase or figure, your
house is on fire
and your children are gone.
When evenings pass as unseen
immaculate ships, and folk –
everyone is suddenly folk – rush to their porches
and lift their faces to this
effervescence of air,
wishing.
            Wishing what?
Just wishing.

SUDDENLY, AT HOME

there was no place we could sit or look
that was not changed to an icon, cursed
with significance: the clothes tree
groping air, the last video, her fish still
nosing the glass, the clocks,
which might as well be moons, the beds,
mouths, and the great great
grandmother staring bleakly from her portrait.
It is just what she might have suspected.

Suddenly at home the cigarette replaces sentences,
its red eye burning in.
In each phrase
the blessèd finch of small talk perishes.
What can you say,
we say, it will take
time, we say, while the mills of thought churn
should have should have and the dog
holds everyone under suspicion.

APRÈS *LA BOHÈME*

After the aesthetic poverty, the bonhomie,
bravado, after the melodies which swell and
spread themselves like easy money,
no one pays the bill
and Mimi dies on four blasts from the horns.
Death is outside in his pickup
which is like a rock. C'mon Mimi
for chrissake.
Now what, brave
bohemians, with the century down to its last
evocative cough and bad
inflammable manuscript,
and an ocean of cold hands rising in the streets?

WHAT KIND OF FOOL AM I?

Bill Evans Solo Sessions 1963

To find your way through the
phrase. Some keys are made of edges some
of broken glass. Bauble. Bangle. You knew the tune
before it was mined. You are the kind of fool
who searches through the rubble of his favourite
things. A note could fall in love off
a cliff down a well. When you fall it
will be forever. Whoever has no house whoever
picks his way and finds
his favourite ledge. Far from April,
far from Paris. Far from his left hand down there
pecking the bright shiny beads. Telling them
off. That kind of fool. Everything
happened to you.

MATÉRIEL

Since his later history is so obscure, it's no wonder he is most remembered for his first bold steps in the areas of sibling rivalry and land use. It should not be forgotten that, although Adam received God's breath, and angels delivered his message, it was Cain who got tattooed – inscribed with the sign which guarantees a sevenfold revenge to be dished out to antagonists. Sometimes translated "Born to Lose."

He was the first to realize there is no future in farming.

How must he have felt, after tilling, sowing, weeding, harvesting, and finally offering his crop, about God's preference for meat? Was God trying to push his prized human creatures further into the fanged romance of chasing and escaping? Was he already in the pocket of the cattle barons? Cain must have scratched and scratched his head before he bashed in his brother's.

He becomes the first displaced person, exiled to the land of Nod, whose etymology, as he probably realized, was already infected with wandering. Then his biography goes underground, rumouring everywhere. Some say he tries farming once again in the hinterland, scratching illegibly at the glacial till before hitting the first road. Some say he fathers a particularly warlike tribe, the Kenites. Some, like Saint Augustine, claim that he takes revenge on agriculture by founding the first cities, rationalizing all his wanderings into streets and tenements, and so charting the course for enclosures and clearances to come. But perhaps his strategy is simpler and more elegant. Perhaps he just thins into his anger, living as a virus in the body politic: the wronged assassin, the anti-farmer, the terrorist tattooed with the promise of sevenfold revenge. Like anyone, he wants to leave his mark.

II. FATES WORSE THAN DEATH

Atrocity
implies an audience of gods.
The gods watched as swiftfooted
godlike Achilles cut behind the tendons of both feet
and pulled a strap of oxhide through
so he could drag the body of Hektor,
tamer of horses, head down in the dust
behind his chariot.
Some were appalled, some not,
having nursed their grudges well, until
those grudges were fine milkfed
adolescents, armed
with automatic weapons. The gods,
and farther off,
the gods before the gods, those who ate
their children and contrived
exquisite tortures in eternity, watched
and knew themselves undead. Such is the loss, such
the wrath of swiftfooted godlike
Achilles, the dumb fucker, that he drags,
up and down, and round and round the tomb
of his beloved, the body of Hektor,
tamer of horses. Atrocity
is never senseless. No. Atrocity is dead ones
locked in sense, forbidden
to return to dust, but scribbled in it,
so that everyone – the gods,
the gods before the gods, the enemy, the absent mothers, all

must read what it is like to live out exile on the earth
without it, to be without recesses, place,
a campsite where the river opens
into the lake, must read
what it means to live against the sun and not to die.
Watch,
he says, alone in the public
newscast of his torment, as he
cuts behind the tendons of both feet,
and pulls a strap of oxhide through,
so he can drag the body that cannot stop being Hektor,
tamer of horses, head down in the dust
behind his chariot, watch
this.

III. THE BASE

Unheard helicopter chop
locks my mind in neutral.
What was it I was supposed to think
as I entered the forbidden country of the base? For this
was not the wisdom I had bargained for –
banality. No orchids of evil
thriving on the phosphorus that leaks
from unexploded shells. No litter of black
ratatats like insoluble hailstones, or fungi
springing up from dead ka-booms.
After nearly forty years of shattered air, I find
not one crystal in the khaki gravel.
Nondescription.

What was Cain thinking
as he wandered here? Whatever
"here" may be, for it has largely been forgotten
by the maps, and also by itself, a large anonymous
amnesia in the middle of New Brunswick.
What shapes occupied the mind
which since has occupied the landscape?
Did he foresee this triumph of enchantment
whereby place itself becomes its camouflage,
surrenders Petersville, Coot Hill, and New
Jerusalem, to take up orders?
Did he anticipate the kingdom of pure policy,
whose only citizens – apart
from coyotes, ravens, moose –

are its police?
Except for graveyards, which have been
preserved, this real estate is wholly owned
and operated by the will, clearcut,
chemicalled and bombed.
Black wires like illegible writing
left everywhere. Ballistics? Baker Dog Charley?
Plastic vials tied to trees at intervals, containing
unknown viscous liquid. In some folktale
I can't conjure, I would steal this potion
and confer great gifts – or possibly destruction –
upon humanity. In a myth
or Wonderland, I'd drink it and become
a native. No thanks.
                              Yet blueberries grow, creeks
sparkle, and an early robin
sings from the scrub. Can a person eat
the berries when they ripen? What kind of fish
thicken in the creeks? During hunting season,
claims the Base Commander, moose and deer
take sanctuary in the impact areas, since no personnel
may enter. Often, late September, you may
see a moose, Jean Paul L'Orignal, perhaps,
sitting on a stump along the border of the base,
huge chin resting on a foreleg,
pondering alternatives: cheerful psychopaths
in psychedelic orange, or a moose-sized replica
of the absurd, ka-boom?

Now I recall
the story of the soldier detailed to attack

an "enemy position," which turned out to be
his grandfather's old farmhouse. Basic Training:
once out of nature he was not about
to get sucked in by some natural seduction
and disgrace himself with tears
or running to the kitchen for an oatmeal cookie.
He made, as we all do, an adjustment.

                       Standing here
still parked in neutral
I'm unable to identify the enemy's position or
sort the evil genii from fallen
farmers, victims and assassins
interpenetrate with vendors and *vendus* in long
chromosomal threads.

                Time to retreat.
Walking back, I try to jump a creek
and sprain my wrist. Pick up your goddamned
feet – . Still, I stop to cut two
pussy-willow branches. Why? Imagined
anti-fasces? Never
was the heaviness of gesture
heavier, nor hope more of a lump,
than trying to imagine that those buds
might, back home in the kitchen, unclench, each fragile hair
pom-pommed with pollen, some day
to open into leaf.

IV. *STRETTO*

Having oversold the spirit, having,
having talked too much of angels, the fool's rush, having the wish,
thicker than a donkey's penis,
holier than o, having the wish
to dress up like the birds,
to dress up like the birds and be and be and be.
Off the hook.
Too good for this world.
Unavailable for comment.
Elsewhere.

*

                    Wonderful Elsewhere, Unspoiled,
Elsewhere as Advertised, Enchanted, Pristine,
Expensive. To lift, voluptuous, each feather cloak
worth fifty thousand finches: to transcend
the food chains we have perched upon and hover – hi there
fans from coast to coast – to beam back dazzling
shots of the stadium, drifting in its cosmos
like a supernova, everywhere the charged
particles of stardom winking and twinkling, o, exponentially
us. As every angel is.

*

Every angle is incestuous.

Agglutinoglomerosis: the inlet choked with algae thriving on

the warmth

imparted by the effluent. *Contermitaminoma*: runoff through

the clearcut takes the topsoil to the river then

out into the bay to coat the coral reef in silt. *Gagaligogo*:

seepage from the landfill finds the water table. *Elugelah*:

the south-

sea island angelized by the first H-blast.

In the dead sea

we will float as stones. Unmortal

*

Unmortality Incorporated.

No shadow. All day

it is noon it is no one. All day

it utters one true sentence jammed

into its period. Nothing is to be allowed

to die but everything gets killed

and then reclassified: the death of its death

makes it an art form. Hang it.

Prohibit the ravens. Prohibit the coyotes.

Prohibit the women with their oils and cloths and

weep weep weeping. Tattoo this extra letter

on the air:

This is what we can do.

Detonation. Heartbeats of the other,

signed, sealed,

delivered. Thunder

eats of its echo eats its vowels smothers its
elf. To strike
hour after hour   the same hour. To dig
redig the gravels that are no one's grave.

*

                   Gravels, aye, tis gravels ye'll gnash
mit muchas gracias and will it please thee sergeant dear to boot
me arse until I hear the mermaids sinking? You know it: tis the
gravel of old rocknroll highroad, me darling sibs, the yellow brick
jornada del muerto. You fancy me far from your minds, wander-
ing lonely as a clod in longlost brotherhood, while your door's
locked and your life's grammatically insured, yet (listen) *scurry
scurry* (Is – That – Only – A – Rat – In – The – Basement – Better
– Phone – Dad – Oh – No – The – Line's – Dead, Mandatory
Lightning Flash) yup, here I am with the hook old chum. Hardly
Fair, what? Now gnash this: beautiful tooth, tooth beautiful.
Repeat: die nacht ist die nacht. How many fucking times do I
have to *Fucking* tell you, me rosasharns? Nayther frahlicher ner
mumbo, nayther oft when on my couch I lie ner *bonny doom* will
lift from these eyes of thine their click clock particles of record
time. *Ammo ergo somme.* We bombs it back to square one, then, o
babes in arms, we bombs square one. Nomine Fat Boy ate Elugelah
ate Alamogordo gravel. Mit click clock lock licht nicht.
Encore.
Die Nacht ist die Nacht.

MEDITATION ON ANTIQUE GLASS

This room, whose windows are waterfalls
in stasis, dreaming in one place, is wrong
for figuring your income tax or poker.
Susceptibility
they say as they teach the light to cry
and introduce hard facts to their first
delicious tremors of metamorphosis:
susceptibility
as though the film were paused at the point of flashing back,
woozy with semiosis: *the rapids are gentle,*
they say, *drink me.* Wrong
for marking essays or making plans.

Nights are worse. Darkness,
as it makes love to the glass, grows thick
and rich, advertising for itself, it whispers
memory muscle, whispers
Guinness is good for you, whispers
loss is its own fur, whispers
once, once
irresistibly.

1. *He rides into town*

already perfect, already filled with nothing. His music is a hawk scream which has been crossed with machine, perhaps eternity's lathe, and fashioned into a horse. His hatbrim is horizon. It is all over. Only the unspeakable trauma which erased his name concerns him. Now it concerns the townsfolk as they scuttle, gutless, behind shopfronts. Two minutes ago their houses were three-dimensional and contained kitchens, not to mention closets. Now the houses, the general store, livery, and sheriff's office are so obviously props that the townsfolk have stopped believing in them before the curtains twitch back into place. Now they are cover awaiting shootout, and the townsfolk are extras waiting to fall, aaargh, from their roofs, and crash, spratinkle tinkle tinkle, through their windows. He rides into town from another genre, from the black star that sucks the depth from everything, a soundless bell tolling. *You should have changed your life*, it says, *done, done, done.* Doesn't even consider that you fixed up the den and took that night class in creative writing.

2. *Their eyes meet*

ah, and there is a satisfying drag on the sprockets, as though the celluloid were suddenly too heavy to turn, as though the projector were sleepy. One violin has been stricken and starts, legato, a drugged smoke alarm, to troll the theme, which the camera catches, tracking left (always left) to take in a quiver of lips. Close-up, close-up, two-shot, their four eyes have begun to unbutton and bud, the strings now ahum, vibrato, zoom zoom zoom they shed the depth of field. Who needs it? The darkness is inhabited, the popcorn is buttered. Their lips approach like shy cats. Her eyes have decided to skinny-dip in his and his in hers: one more micro-zoom and they dive, leaving the rest of their faces behind to nuzzle and rub, attempting to smudge the irregular line between them. And the eyes? Are swimming with us, dolphins, in the darkness, which is rich and viscous, the lake of tears we've been waiting for.

and settle into our bodies, waiting for the lights to dim so we can feel ourselves falling, this is the best part, feel ourselves falling into a safer kind of sleep, an elaborate parkland of carefully prepared surprises. As the curtains begin to part, *lingerie*, we can see through them to the screen, which has begun to flicker into being. Will the plot matter? Of course not. Movies have been sent to us to make up for the bathroom mirror, with its rigid notion of representation, and the family, with its chain-link semantic net. Here we feel ideas wriggle into costume and images reach toward us out of light. Soon their logos will appear – the winged horse in the symmetrical cosmos, perhaps, or shifting constellations that swirl into an O. Everything will be incarnate, *in camera*, anything can be a star.

ODE TO MY CAR

As if. As if it oiled your idle
notions, machined,
massaged them till there never was no
clunk no hand me that spanner no
crank 'er over.
As if motor were simply the syrinx of speed as if
movie movie all you ever have to pay is your attention, focus
on the docudrama in the windshield, stay tuned
to the hummingbird who hums in the accelerator, in the cylinders
the six brave heart attacks are singing and the clutch
performs the sigh with which the lovers shift into
                                        more comfortable
positions:
            there.
Something has come from nothing, as if
a handful of its blackberries had been
gathered. Something in a tooth
desires to speak in tongues. Something in a consonant
attends its vowels, as if
minuet. Synchromesh.
Momentum. Here lies the precise
mystery of transmission.

The tools of music: this is where it first
emerged from noise and how it
stays in touch with clutter
and how it gets back to the heart –
that single-stroke kachunker with its grab, give,
grab. He is bringing the kitchen,
the workshop, screwing wingnuts and attaching
brackets, placing the pedals like accelerators,
setting up the stands for snare and high hat like decapitated
wading birds. How music will make itself walk
into the terrible stunned air behind the shed
where all the objects looked away. Now the hollow bodies,
their blank moons tilted *just asking for it*, and back and
back to the time you missed the step
and dropped the baby and your heart leapt out
to catch it, for all those accidents that might have
and that happened he floats the ride and then
suspends the crash above the wreckage like its flat
burnished bell.
Unsheathes the brushes that can shuffle through the grass
or pitter like small rain. All this hardware to recall
the mess you left back home
and bring it to the music
and get back to the heart.
He sits on the stool
in the middle of your life
and waits to feel the beat. To speak it
and keep it. Here we go.

Their behaviour is acoustically mysterious . . . we get
fundamentals being pitched a third or a fourth deeper, as if the
air column were projected back, in imagination, to the true apex
of the cone-bore, which is in most cases several inches beyond
the reed (down the player's throat, as it were).
– Anthony Baines, *Woodwind Instruments and Their History*

Lying in its case, the alto sax looks brash, *nouveau riche*, a gold
tooth. Pick it up, heft it, plonk the keys down with a sound like
whumping the top of a beer bottle. You could play this thing,
man, it's just a kazoo with buttons. Follow the action as you press
this key or that, watching the force reverse over a see-saw hinge
or torque around the cylinder to pop a hole open or closed: *mech-*
anism: it's a fantastic insect, the elegance of niftiness rather than
refinement. So blow. The sax isn't going to transform your breath
like other instruments but magnify it, reaching back down your
throat to amplify its possibilities, giving prominence to neglected
dialects like the honk, the cough, the hum, and even (Archie
Shepp) the last gasp. It does not concern itself with angels, as the
flute, nor with the dead like Dante, modernism, and the cello. It
does not even imitate or extend the human voice as the violin is
said to do. The sax is equipment singing – our equipment: a trou-
bling of air which addresses us, the dying, from our own respira-
tory systems. Its idiom is breath, unrelieved of the deplorable
burdens of sex and work. It has the richness of a muffler in its last
days, an overloaded ferry on a muddy river. You may hear your
father's phlegmy old Chev or the soft honk of Trumpeter Swans
over miles of high prairie. You may hear *soupe du zoo*. You will

always hear the sob in the note, the hollow sob which comes from the lung, the womb of voice. The sob that will gather the unsay-able without cashing it in on lyric silver. When the wind blows (Lao-tzu) there is only wind. When the sax blows there is only wind and the whole goddamned human condition. Mortality's exhaust pipe. Ready for nothing.

1. *Knife*

who comes to the table fresh
from killing the pig, edge
of edges,
entry into zip.
                    Knife
who can swim as its secret
through the dialogue or glimmer
in a kitchen drawer. Who first appeared
in God's hand to divide
the day from the night, then the sheep
from the goats, then from the other
sheep, then from their comfortable
fleeces. Nothing sinister in this except
it had to happen and it was the first
to have to. The imperative
mood. For what we about to take
we must be grateful.

2. *Fork*

a touch of kestrel,
of Chopin, your hand with its fork
hovers above the plate, or punctuates
a proposition. This is the devil's favourite
instrument, the fourfold
family of prongs: Hard Place,
Rock, Something You Should Know,
and For Your Own Good. At rest,
face up, it says,
please, its tines
pathetic as an old man's fingers on a bed.
Face down it says
anything that moves.

3. *Spoon*

whose eloquence
is tongueless, witless, fingerless,
an absent egg.
Hi Ho, sing knife and fork, as off they go,
chummy as good cop and bad cop,
to interrogate the supper. Spoon waits
and reflects your expression,
inverted, in its tarnished moonlight. It knows
what it knows. It knows hunger
from the inside
out.

ABANDONED TRACKS: AN ECLOGUE

As always, I walk the ties, trying to
syncopate my step to their awkward
interval. It's hot. At some age, six or eight,
the distance matches the length of your leg exactly,
you can march to town in two-four time. Now
Cow Vetch and Mustard get in the way
and hide the ties. "Sleepers." Watch your step.
A Goldfinch lands on a rail, then a White-tail Dragonfly,
its pause a half-beat between darts. The heat
is tired in its bones, exhausted by absent thunder
like a couple trying to get pregnant, dragging their sad
much-discussed ass to bed.
Back in Moderns, Dr. Reaney led us
into Yoknapatawpha County. He had been there. "Remember
it is *hot*; stick all that past in a pot
and set it on the stove." Bindweed and Wild Grape
curl around the rails, tendrils, tentacles, the tracks
in the distance with their old
Parkinsonian shake. Around my head
the comic-book sign for dizziness is being etched
by deerflies. Quentin Compson
hungers for his sister, who will later bear a daughter,
also Quentin, who will steal the cash,
her own, from her ordinary, evil
uncle, and run off with the red-tied carny-man. Hawkweed
                                                            and Daisies
sharpen their hardihood on gravel. The spikes,
once hammered like cold bolts from the blue,

are loosening. Feel this –
a wobbly tooth. We loved the old train, really, it
would take an afternoon's mosquito and cicada hum,
pre-amplify it, put a big bass underneath, we'd feel it
in the air the way, I guess, a horse can sense an earthquake
                                        coming, we'd
drop everything – berry pails, books – and run down
to the tracks, Luke in manic overdrive because
June was busting out all over and we'd all turned dog. We'd stand
throbbing in its aura, waving; the blunt-faced locomotive,
a few tanker cars full of polysyllabic stuff,
the caboose with maybe a reciprocating wave, the throb
thinning to the whine of iron wheels on iron rails.
To be next door to violence, that dreadful
blundering. It was fun. It was cathartic. Now it's like
single-point perspective had let go, shattering into the tip
tilt hop of the Yellow warbler's pointillist attention
in the Rock elm. So much intricate
tenacity. Milkweed with its lavish
muted blooms, the milk that feeds the larvae
of Monarch butterflies and makes them
poisonous to birds. When the train ran over Luke
it was too dumb to pause or blow its whistle, probably
never saw him there between the tracks or heard us
shouting into the electric deafness of the moment.
Well. That spot is occupied by Bladder campion now.
With its cheeks puffed out behind its blooms, it's like
a gang of Dizzy Gillespies and the final
freeze-frame for the story: except, somehow
Luke survived the train, and then the shock,
which also should have killed him.

Back from the vet, stitched,
still groggy from the drugs, he sensed the old throb
troubling the air and struggled growling to his feet
ready for round two. Talk about dumb. It was funny
and appalling, and we knew, wincing at each other,
that it wasn't just our true intrepid friend
we were appalled by. When the Monarchs hatch
they'll feed and flit and pollinate their hosts,
by accident, and after an infinitude of flits
wind up precisely in one Mexican valley. Some thoughts
live in the mind as larvae, some as the milk they feed on,
some as the wanderings which are the way. Heal-all,
Yarrow. Everything the tracks
have had no use for's happening
between them.

TO DANCELAND

No one is ever happier than when they're dancing.
   – Margaret McKay

South through bumper crops we are driving to Danceland, barley
oats, canola, wheat, thick as a beaver pelt, but late, she said,
late, since June had been so cold already we were deep
in August and still mostly green so it was nip
and tuck with frost and somewhere between Nipawin and
                                        Tisdale finally
I found the way to say, um, I can't dance
you know, I can't dance don't ask me
why I am driving like a fool to Danceland having flunked it
twenty-seven years ago in the kitchen where my mother,
bless her, tried to teach me while I passively resisted,
doing the jerk-step while she tried to slow, slow, quick quick
slow between the table and the fridge, her face fading
like someone trying to start a cranky Lawnboy
                                        nevertheless,
                        step by sidestep
we are driving down the grid, Swainson's hawks occurring every
thirty hydro poles, on average
                        to Danceland
where the dancefloor floats on rolled horsehair
and the farmers dance with their wives even though it is
                                        not Chicago
where the mirror ball blesses everyone with flecks from
                        another, less rigorous, dimension
where the Westeel granary dances with the weathervane,

the parent with the child, the John Deere with the mortgage
where you may glimpse occasional coyote lopes and gopher hops
where the dark may become curious and curl one long arm

                                                    around us
as we pause for a moment, and I think about my mother and her
wishes in that kitchen, then
we feed ourselves to the world's most amiable animal,
in Danceland.

V

Sometimes a voice – have you heard this? –
wants not to be voice any longer, wants something
whispering between the words, some
rumour of its former life. Sometimes, even
in the midst of making sense or conversation it will
hearken back to breath, or even farther,
to the wind, and recognize itself
as troubled air, a flight path still
looking for its bird.
                                    I'm thinking of us up there
shingling the boathouse roof. That job is all
off balance – squat, hammer, body skewed
against the incline, heft the bundle,
daub the tar, squat. Talking,
as we always talked, about not living
past the age of thirty with its
labyrinthine perils: getting hooked,
steady job, kids, business suit. Fuck that. The roof
sloped upward like a take-off ramp
waiting for Evel Knievel, pointing into open sky. Beyond it
twenty feet or so of concrete wharf before
the blue-black water of the lake. Danny said
that he could make it, easy. We said
never. He said case of beer, put up
or shut up. We said
asshole. Frank said first he should go get our beer
because he wasn't going to get it paralysed or dead.
Everybody got up, taking this excuse

to stretch and smoke and pace the roof
from eaves to peak, discussing gravity
and Steve McQueen, who never used a stunt man, Danny's
life expectancy, and whether that should be a case
of Export or O'Keefe's. We knew what this was –
ongoing argument to fray
the tedium of work akin to filter vs. plain,
stick shift vs. automatic, condom vs.
pulling out in time. We flicked our butts toward the lake
and got back to the job. And then, amid the squat,
hammer, heft, no one saw him go. Suddenly he
wasn't there, just his boots
with his hammer stuck inside one like a heavy-headed
flower. Back then it was bizarre that,
after all that banter, he should be so silent,
so inward with it just to
run off into sky. Later I thought,
cool. Still later I think it makes sense his voice should
sink back into breath and breath
devote itself to taking in whatever air
might have to say on that short flight between the roof
and the rest of his natural life.

LIFT

To stand with mind akimbo where the wind
riffles the ridge. Slow,
slow jazz: it must begin
before the instrument with bones
dreaming themselves hollow and the dusk
rising in them like a sloth
ascending. Moon,
night after night rehearsing shades of pause
and spill, sifting into reed beds,
silvering the fine hairs on your arms, making
rhythm out of light and nothing, making
months. What have I ever made of life or it
of me, all I ever asked for was to be remembered
constantly by everything I ever touched. So much
to relinquish there's a housing crisis
in eternity. What I need now is two square
yards of night to wrap up in,
a chrysalis from which, who knows
how many epochs later,
something – maybe dotted, maybe ragged,
maybe dun – unfolds. Something quick.
Something helpful to the air.

But, however,
on the other hand.
Not gravity, that irresistible embrace,
but its photograph, packed in your bag
with too many shirts. Drag
wants to dress the nakedness of speed, to hold clothes
in the slipstream until body reincarnates, then
it will be sorry, won't it?
Yes it will. It will be as sorry as the
square of its upward urge.

                          When I approached the edge
it seemed one gentle waft
would carry me across, the brief lilt
of a Horned Lark up from roadside gravel
into the adjacent field.

                  However,
on the other hand. It occurred to me that,
unlike Horned Larks, who are imagination,
I was mostly memory, which,
though photogenic and nutritious, rich
with old-time goodness, is notoriously
heavier than air.

Once past the street lights I miss it,
"poised" at the spruce tip, "floating"
in the pond, the way it gathered longing into moths
and kept reality from overdosing on its own sane
self. It seems the dead,
who would otherwise be dressing up in moonstuff, blending
with the birch to be both here
and not here, lose interest in us and descend
below the reach of roots. The hydro wires
are hydro wires, the streets are streets, the houses
full of television. On tombstones
names and dates are fading into vague
depressions, or else (not impossibly)
we have forgotten how to read. Who can say
if these are names or simply the effect
of weather on the stone, and if they were,
what possible connection they would have to persons
rumoured to have once gone to and fro? No one,
says Yeats, but no one
is born at this phase, whose only
incarnation is the dark. Possibly this is the hole
the Fool (phase 28) falls into –

                              so I reflect as,
taking the path among the evergreens,
I lose my way – the way I know like the back
of my own hand – which is busy fending off
the clutchings of the spruce – the very spruce I planted
forty years ago – and wind up

besnaggled in the dark and many-needled wood
which is mythless
which is pathless
which is mine.

SONG FOR THE SONG OF THE COYOTE

Moondogs, moondogs,
tell me the difference between tricks
and wisdom, hunting
and grieving.
I listen in the tent, my ear
to the ground. There is a land even
more bare than this one, without sage,
or prickly pear, or greasewood. A land
that can only wear its scars, every crater
etched. Riverless. Treeless. You sing to its thin
used-up light, yips and floated tremolos and screams,
sculpted barks like fastballs of packed
air. Echoes that articulate the buttes and coulees and dissolve
into the darkness, which is always listening.

LOAD

We think this
the fate of mammals – to bear, be born,
be burden, to carry our own bones
as far as we can and know the force that earths us
intimately. Sometimes, while I was reading,
Sam would bestow one large paw on my foot,
as if to support my body
while its mind was absent – mute
commiseration, load to load, a message
like the velvet heaviness which comes
to carry you deliciously
asleep.
          One morning
on the beach at Point Pelee, I met
a White-throated Sparrow so exhausted from the flight
across Lake Erie it just huddled in itself
as I crouched a few yards off.
I was thinking of the muscles in that grey-white breast,
pectoralis major powering each downstroke,
pectoralis minor with its rope-and-pulley tendon
reaching through the shoulder to the
top side of the humerus to haul it up again;
of the sternum with the extra keel it has evolved to
anchor all that effort, of the dark wind
and the white curl on he waves below, the slow dawn
and the thickening shoreline.

                              I wanted
very much to stroke it, and recalling
several terrors of my brief
and trivial existence, didn't.

ICARUS

isn't sorry. We do not find him
doing penance, writing out the golden mean for all
eternity, or touring its high schools to tell student bodies
not to do what he done
done. Over and over he rehearses flight
and fall, tuning his moves, entering
with fresh rush into the mingling of the air
with spirit. This is his practice
and his prayer: to be translated into air, as air
with each breath enters lungs,
then blood. He feels resistance gather in his stiff
strange wings, angles his arms to shuck the sweet lift
from the drag, runs the full length
of a nameless corridor, his feet striking the paving stones
less and less heavily, then
they're bicycling above the ground,
a few shallow beats and he's up,
he's out of the story and into the song.

At the melting point of wax, which now he knows
the way Doug Harvey knows the blue line,
he will back-beat to create a pause, hover for maybe fifty
hummingbird heartbeats and then
lose it, tumbling into freefall, shedding feathers
like a lover shedding clothes. He may glide
in the long arc of a Tundra swan or pull up sharp
to Kingfisher into the sea which bears his name. Then,
giving it the full Ophelia, drown.

On the shore
the farmer ploughs his field, the dull ship
sails away, the poets moralize about our
unsignificance. But Icarus is thinking tremolo and
backflip, is thinking
next time with a half-twist
and a tuck and isn't
sorry.

*

Repertoire, technique. The beautiful contraptions bred from inge-
nuity and practice, and the names by which he claims them, into
which – lift-off, loop-the-loop – they seem to bloom. Icarus could
write a book. Instead he will stand for hours in that musing half-
abstracted space, watching. During fall migrations he will often
climb to the edge of a north-south running ridge where the
soaring hawks find thermals like naturally occurring laughter,
drawing his eyebeam up an unseen winding stair until they
nearly vanish in the depth of sky. Lower down, Merlins slice the
air with wings that say crisp crisp, precise as sushi chefs, while
Sharp-shins alternately glide and flap, hunting as they go, each
line break poised, ready to pivot like a point guard or Robert
Creeley. Icarus notices how the Red-tails and Broadwings sepa-
rate their primaries to spill a little air, giving up just enough lift to
break their drag up into smaller trailing vortices. What does this
remind him of? He thinks of the kind of gentle teasing that can
dissipate a dark mood so it slips off as a bunch of skirmishes and
quirks. Maybe that. Some little gift to acknowledge the many
claims of drag and keep its big imperative at bay. Icarus knows all
about that one too.

In the spring he heads for a slough and makes himself a blind out of wolf willow and aspen, then climbs inside to let the marsh-mind claim his thinking. The soft splashdowns of Scaup and Bufflehead, the dives which are simple shrugs and vanishings; the Loon's wing, thin and sharp for flying in the underwater world, and the broad wing of the Mallard, powerful enough to break the water's grip with one sweep, a guffaw which lifts it straight up into the air. Icarus has already made the mistake of trying this at home, standing on a balustrade in the labyrinth and fanning like a manic punkah, the effort throwing him backward off his perch and into a mock urn which the Minotaur had, more than once, used as a pisspot. Another gift of failure. Now his watching is humbler, less appropriative, a thoughtless thinking amid fly drone and dragonfly dart. Icarus will stay in the blind until his legs cramp up so badly that he has to move. He is really too large to be a foetus for more than an hour. He unbends creakily, stretches, and walks home, feeling gravity's pull upon him as a kind of wealth.

*

Sometimes Icarus dreams back into his early days with Daedalus in the labyrinth. Then he reflects upon the Minotaur, how seldom they saw him – did they ever? – while they shifted constantly from no-place to no-place, setting up false campsites and leaving decoy models of themselves. Sometimes they would come upon these replicas in strange postures, holding their heads in their laps or pointing to their private parts. Once they discovered two sticks stuck like horns in a decoy's head, which Daedalus took to be the worst of omens. Icarus was not so sure.

For today's replay he imagines himself sitting in a corridor reflecting on life as a minotaur (*The* Minotaur) while waiting for his alter ego to come bumbling by. They were, he realizes, both children of technology – one its *enfant terrible*, the other the rash adolescent who, they will always say, should never have been given a pilot's license in the first place. What will happen when they finally meet? Icarus imagines dodging like a Barn swallow, throwing out enough quick banter to deflect his rival's famous rage and pique his interest. How many minotaurs does it take to screw in a light bulb? What did the Queen say to the machine?

Should he wear two sticks on his head, or save that for later? He leaps ahead to scenes out of the Hardy Boys and Tom Sawyer. They will chaff and boast and punch each other on the arm. They will ridicule the weird obsessions of their parents. As they ramble, cul-de-sacs turn into secret hideouts and the institutional corridors take on the names of birds and athletes. They discover some imperfections in the rock face, nicks and juts which Daedalus neglected to chisel off, and which they will use to climb, boosting and balancing each other until they fall off. Together they will scheme and imagine. Somehow they will find a way to put their brute heads in the clouds.

was a moon,
before it fisted itself into otherness inside the
body of the earth, bulbed,
broke out on its own,
there was no second gravity and no
dark art of reflection. The sun owned
all the media and it occurred to no one to resist
its health-and-fitness
propaganda. Whatever a thing was,
that was it, no ifs or
airspace. Place was obese
before the moon was moon, so full of itself
there was no leaving home, and so
no dwelling in it either. Longing was short
and sedentary. Blues were red. No sweet tug
toward our manic possibilities, no wistful,
sidelong, inner, sly, no alder branch
hung above the smooth rush of the snow-fed river like the
stray wisp hovering against your cheek which
in a moment you will tuck back
into tidiness, no such stretched connection before
moon was moon. No way to deflect the light
away from photosynthesis and into alcohol
and film. Each night
was the same night, and fell formlessly,
with no imagination,
and without you in it.

That things should happen
twice, and place
share the burden of remembering. Home,
the first cliché. We say it
with aspiration as the breath
opens to a room of its own (a bed,
a closet for the secret self), then closes
on a hum. Home. Which is the sound of time
braking a little, growing slow and thick as the soup
that simmers on the stove. Abide,
abode. Pass me that plate,
the one with the hand-painted *habitant*
sitting on a log. My parents bought it
on their honeymoon – see? Dated on the bottom,
1937. He has paused to smoke his pipe, the tree
half-cut and leaning. Is he thinking where
to build his cabin or just idling his mind
while his pipe smoke mingles with the air? A bird,
or something (it is hard to tell), hangs overhead.
Now it's covered by your grilled cheese sandwich.

Part two, my interpretation. The leaning tree
points home, then
past home into real estate and its innumerable
Kodak moments: kittens, uncles,
barbecues. And behind those scenes the heavy
footstep on the stair, the face locked
in the window frame, things that happen

and keep happening, reruns
of family romance. And the smudged bird? I say it's
a Yellow Warbler who has flown
from winter habitat in South America to nest here
in the clearing. If we catch it, band it,
let it go a thousand miles away it will be back
within a week. How?
Home is what we know
and know we know, the intricately
feathered nest. Homing
asks the question.

You may openly
endorse the air, but if you can't
be canny, and, come to that, apt,
chances are you won't
get off the ground.
                  We audited
our raw materials: a lawn chair,
an abandoned stroller and a snarl
of coat hangers – necks, hooks, elbows –
wrangling. Handles and
clock hands. How-to's on migration guided
by the stars, by the earth's
electromagnetism, by the ultra-low groans
spoken by the mountains. Now
we needed duct tape, a philosophy of feathers
and a plan: what to
fall for, gracefully,
and without too much
deliberation, how to mix
the mysticism with the ash and live
next door to nothing,
and with art.

Another gravity. I am on my way
to the bathroom, the dream in my head still
struggling not to die into the air, when my bare feet step
into a pool of moonlight on the kitchen floor and turn,
effortlessly, into fish. All day surviving in the grim purdah
of my work socks wishing only to be kissed by cold
equivocal light, now they swim off,
up, singing old bone river, hunched-up toes
and gormless ankles growing
sleek and silver, old bone river,
gather me back.
On pause in my kitchen,
footless, I think of them up there among the night fliers –
Snow geese, swans, songbirds –
navigating by the stars and earth's own
brainwaves. How early radar techs discovered
ghostly blotches on their screens and,
knowing they weren't aircraft – theirs
or ours – called them angels. Back in my dream
the old lady who sells popcorn has been fading in my arms
as I run through its corridors and lobbies, taking her
empty weight through foyers, antechambers,
vestibules, a whole aerobics class completely deaf
inside its trance of wellness, my old
popcorn lady dwindling to a feather boa,
then a scarf of smoke. A gravity
against the ground, a love
which summons no one home

and calls things to their water-souls. On the tide flats
shore birds feed and bustle, putting on fat
for the next leg of the long
throw south. When a cold front
crosses the Fundy coast, they test it
with their feathers, listening to its muscular
northwesterlies, deciding when to give their bodies
to that music and be swept,
its ideal audience, far out over the Atlantic. The face
in the bathroom mirror looks up
just as I arrive, a creature that has
caught me watching and is watching back. Around us
wind has risen, rushes in the foliage,
tugs at the house.

SNOW MOON

(January: Fredericton, New Brunswick)

With no name
and no mask. Not the dusty rock,
not the goddess, not the decor of romance,
not the face. Express from infinity
it arrives in a flood of cold desire like a
tooth, like a voracious
reader. The snow wakes singing, its empty angels
filling with invisible silica, quickening
to fly off as Snowy owls.
The mind of winter.
                    This moon who refuses to defer,
whose light is the death of fire and the silence of the loon,
whose song can snap off ears.

KINDS OF BLUE #41 (FAR HILLS)

Viola, cello, double bass, the distances
deepen and address us. What is this language
we have almost learnt, or nearly not
forgotten, with its soft
introspective consonants, its drone
of puréed names? It says we ought to mourn
but not to grieve, it says that even loss
may be a place, it says
repose. The eye would like to fold its rainbow
like a fan, and quit
discriminating between this and that,
and indigo and mauve,
and go there. Once,
while sleeping in my down-filled sleeping bag
I dreamt of Eiders, diving
and diving into the dark Arctic Ocean, and woke
bereft and happy, my whole mind
applauding.

Before it can stop itself, the mind
has leapt up inferences, crag to crag,
the obvious arpeggio. Where there is a doorbell
there must be a door – a door
meant to be opened from inside.
Door means house means – wait a second –
but already it is standing on a threshold previously
known to be thin air, gawking. The Black Spruce
point to it: clarity,
melting into ordinary morning, true
north. Where the sky is just a name,
a way to pitch a little tent in space and sleep
for five unnumbered seconds.

CAMBER

That rising curve, the fine line
between craft and magic where we
travel uphill without effort, where anticipation,
slipping into eros,
                              summons the skin. When you
say "you" with that inflection something stirs
inside the word, echo
infected with laugh. One night O., gazing at the moon
as usual, encountered K. as he was trying to outwalk
bureaucracy. Yes, they said, let's. If it is
possible to translate poetry, then,
what isn't?

GLIDE

Sometimes the eye brims
over with desire and pours
into its flight path:

this is gaze, and glide
is when the body follows,
flowing into river, when the heart,

turning the word "forever"
into plainsong,
learns to purr, knowing

the most important
lesson of grade four
is the blank but pointed

page, the pure wish that we
sharpen into dart and send
skimming the desks and out

the window, through the schoolyard
with its iron jungle gym, across
the traffic we must always

stop and look both
ways for, meanwhile, gazing
at us from its prehistoric perch, a small

but enterprising lizard
is about to launch itself
into the warm arms of the Mesozoic afternoon.

> *We talk because we are mortal.*
> — Octavio Paz

And because we aren't gods,
or close to gods,
we sing. Your breath steps
boldly into lift to feel that other breath
breathing inside it: Summertime, Amazing Grace.

                                        And when it stops
you sense that something fold back
into air to leave you listening,
lonely as a post. Shall we call this angel?
Shall we call it animal, or elf? Most of us
are happy with a brief
companionable ghost who joins us in the shower or
behind the wheel. Blue Moon, Hound Dog, Life
Is Like a Mountain Railroad. When your voice
decides to quit its day job, which is mostly
door-to-door, to take its little sack of sounds
and pour them into darkness, with its
unembodied barks and murmurs, its refusal
to name names, its disregard for sentences,
for getting there on time,
or getting there,
or getting.

HOVER

What goes up
improvises, makes itself a shelf out of nowt,
out of ether and work, ushering the air, backstroke
after backstroke, underneath
the earth turns and you
don't, and don't,
and don't: O
who do you think you are so
hugely paused, pissing off both
gravity and time,
refusing to be born into the next
inexorable instant?
We wait in our
pocket of held breath, secretly
cheering you on.
Do it for us.

HANG TIME

Some say it's the blip
produced when missing heartbeats – from the terrible half-
expected phone call or the child who wasn't where you
thought she was – sneak back into flow
and get assimilated. Some say
sunspots. Either way, evidence of eddies
in the ever-rolling stream, a gift to the wingless which
increases our capacity to yearn
and taste for tricks. You have a strange expression
on your face, as though
walking a long corridor of doors, trying each one,
1324, No Entry, 1326, one of these
has got to be the way up
to the roof.

TURBULENCE

There is at present no precise definition of turbulence, although
we can say that velocity exhibits finite oscillations of a random
character that cause irregularities in the path of a suspended par-
ticle of scale comparable with the lengths that determine the
kinematics of the mean motion, we can say
vortices
       eddies
            coefficient of drag
                   we can say agitated
particles, we can say at present no,
at present there is precious
deformation, the ferocity exhibits final
oscar nominations of those random
characters, the claws, irregulars, the plaths of suspense,
the partisans of sale, the compost rabble
and the lynx that undermines, we can say
killer statics of mean motion, dwarf diseases,
all the eds and eddies and the sad
co-fishermen of drag, the agitated
hearts and hearticles of what
we cannot say there is at present.

Leaving home loves homing: you can scrawl that
in the washroom, carve it in the old oak, carry it
inside your carry-on
luggage. When I comprehend the tragi-comic
turns and nude scenes of their long
romance it's going to explain
plenty, from the strange behaviours of the dead
to why I do the dishes happily
and badly. In the cemetery by the sea
the Chestnut-backed chickadees kibitz and flit, Yew
to Douglas-fir to Weeping
birch. They must be the selves
of dear departed ones, still full of just
a minute while I put the kettle on and doctors,
what do they know. Wearing their
tangibility and pluck, their fresh
capacity for being sorely missed. Wearing the way
you sang off key like a new plaid
sports coat. While those others, the cherished
and exquisite rumours of the spirit, soar through our
imaginations with the dumb nonchalance
of albatrosses. Sometimes I listen
much too closely to the crows,
especially those who perch on the neon signs
and rooftops of the plaza, where they
parley in the voices of burnt
oboes, boldface and illegible.
They know something. Something

about scavenging and shopping and the interwoven
deerpaths of desire. Something about loss
made visible. Homing loves leaving
home. When I comprehend that wing.
When I run off with that heartless music.

PLUMMET

Simple.
Under one wing you take the thousand thousand
thuds of your heart, under the other
a lifetime paying taxes to the wind –
and clench.
Where there was flibbertigibbetry of feather, now
          the quick of existence in a fist.
Where there was phrase, phrase, nickel-and-diming it to stay
one breath ahead, now
          you take the full stop in your teeth
          the plumb bob
          the bomb.
Where there were unnumbered paths of air, now
          the one shaft of your plunge, whose walls
          are the shrieks of your old nemesis, gravity

          bursting into bloom.

SOMETIMES A VOICE (2)

Sometimes a voice – have you heard this? –
wants not to be voice any longer and this longing
is the worst of longings. Nothing
assuages. Not the curry-comb of conversation,
not the dog-eared broken
satisfactions of the blues. It huddles in the lungs
and won't come out. Not for the Mendelssohn Choir
constructing habitable spaces in the air, not for Yeats
intoning "Song of the Old Mother" to an ancient
microphone. It curls up in its cave
and will not stir. Not for the gentle quack
of saxophone, not for raven's far-calling
croak. Not for *oh* the lift of poetry, or *ah*
the lover's sigh, or *um* the phrase's lost
left shoe. It tucks its nose beneath its brush
and won't. If her whisper tries
to pollinate your name, if a stranger yells
hey kid, va t'en chez toi to set another music
going in your head it simply
enters deafness. Nothing
assuages. Maybe it is singing
high in the cirque, burnishing itself
against the rockwall, maybe it is
clicking in the stones turned by the waves like faceless
dice. Have you heard this? – in the hush
of invisible feathers as they urge the dark,
stroking it toward articulation? Or the moment

when you know it's over and the nothing which you
have to say is falling all around you, lavishly,
pouring its heart out.

FINGER POINTING AT THE MOON

> *We come from a hidden ocean, and we go to an unknown ocean.*
> – Antonio Machado

Everything you think of has already happened
and been sung by the sea. We were hiking
along the coast, with the hush and boom of surf
in our ears, on a trail so wet it was mostly
washouts strung together, forcing us
to find fresh ways around, teetery
and nimble, until I thought, yes,
the real agenda of this so-called trail
is not to lead us through this sopping biomass
but into it, with the surf
as soundtrack. Everything you think, it sang,
has already happened and been sung in long
confessional sighs and softly
crashing dactyls, wash, rinse,
wash, useless to resist. Each wave,
having travelled incognito through its ocean,
surges up to rush the rock, Homer was here, and perish,
famous and forgotten. On the beach
the back-drag clicks the stones and pebbles
on each other, a death rattle that is somehow soothing, somehow
music, some drum kit from the far side of the blues
where loss begins to shuffle. It's O.K. to disappear. Off balance,
I'm trying to hop from stepping stone to stone
when I flash back forty years to my friend's
younger sister sitting in the boat,

trailing her fingers as we row out to the raft, how she gazes,
pouring herself into water as its depth
pours into her. I remember
being embarrassed she'd been caught out
having an inner life and rowed hard for the raft
where summer fun was waiting with its brawny cannonballs
and swan dives. I think each memory is lit
by its own small moon – a snowberry,
a mothball, a dime – which regulates its tides
and longings. Next time I am going to lift the oars
so we can watch the droplets fall back,
hidden ocean into unknown ocean,
while we drift. I will need a word
to float there, some empty blue-green bottle
that has lost its label. When we lose the trail entirely,
or it feeds us to the rain forest,
what will we be like? Probably not the Winter wren,
whose impossible song is the biography of Buddha,
then Mary Shelley, then your no-good Uncle Ray.
Not the Cat-tail Moss
which hangs in drapes and furs the fallen logs in lavish
sixties shag. I think we come here so our words
can fail us, get humbled by the stones, drown,
be lost forever, then come back
as beach glass, polished and anonymous,
knowing everything. Knowing everything they
think of has already happened, everything they think of has
already happened and been sung, knowing
everything they think of has already happened and been sung,
in all its tongues and metres, and to no one,
by the sea.

WINTER SOLSTICE MOON: AN ECLOGUE

(December: Pacific Rim National Park)

Full moon falling on Christmas eve: I wondered,
as we carried our supplies – wine, rain gear, gifts –
from the car to the cabin, whether everything was
about to get conscripted into either family life
or lunacy. We put
the perishables in the fridge,
walked out on the beach: in the east
the blacker blackness of the mountains, already backlit
by the moon, and lower down each cabin's roof
outlined in lights, reminding everyone that this
was supposed to be the feast of homes
and homebodies, the time to bring a tree indoors
and charm its boreal heart with bric-a-brac,
to make ourselves so interesting its needles would forget
the roots they left behind. On the wet
corrugated sand the lights were smeared and
rippled, an elaborate film noir effect,
an opening sequence into which a cop car,
like an urban orca, should intrude. To the west
ocean was a far roar under its hush-hush
in the sand, a giant with a lisp.

I was thinking of the house we'd left
huddled darkly round its
turned-down furnace, one missing tooth
in the block's electric smile. How much

we ask of them, that they articulate
the space around us into stanzas,
pauses in the flow which gather time,
or rather where time, slightly pregnant,
might gather if it chose; that they should be the bodies
of our bodies and the spirit's husk
against the hypothermia which dogs it,
a.k.a. the dreads; that they be resolute yet intimate, insulated,
pest-free, dry, well-founded in the earth but airy,
fire in the belly and a good deep well attached to copper
plumbing, CSA approved; that they should be
possessed of character but not by ghosts, and not
the sort of character who wakes you
in the middle of the night and suddenly
needs money; that they should shed the rain and keep the wind
from blowing out the candle flame of talk, the bedtime stories,
murmurings, the small redundant phrases with which one voice
solaces another.
And when it goes awry – the cracks the bills the noise the
drains the silences the bugs – to take the blame and sit there,
stoically, on the market while new dreamers sniff the air
and poke their noses into closets,
hatching their improbable plots.

We walked through soft mist,
filling our ears with the ocean's boom
and whisper. Is it the listening that loosens,
letting its knots go, or the voice,
saying those great unsayings to itself until
ovation on the inside equals ovation out? And rain forest,
I thought as we turned back at the cliff,

must be the way it gets translated into plants,
who remember water with each rounded,
downward gesture.
                    Then the moon. Over the mountain it hung
and roiled inside itself,
pure style which took the scene aslant, selecting
the bristle of frost on the drift logs, the patch
of duct tape on my boot, the whites of your eyes,
leaving whatever was not glimmering in deeper shadow,
uninhabited. Can you recall
those nights we spent learning from the wolves to be
the tooth and tongue of darkness, how to hunt
and howl? Me neither. Now that howl's
inverted in us, the long o of *alone*. The wolves
are dogs. The sun says *here*, the moon says
nowhere, the nameless moon
that sheds the blunt domesticating myths
the way a mirror utterly forgets you
when you leave the bathroom, the empty moon
soliciting our ghosts, calling on them to leave home,
that gilded cage, that theme park of the human.

But the sea was gazing back, its look
rich with tumult and the possibility of huge hearts
sounding the depths. Between them
otherworldliness is quickened. One theory –
my favourite – goes that once the earth and moon were one,
spinning monthlessly in space, and somehow –
                              whether by asteroid
or apple, *différance*, tabu – they broke up and the moon,
newly fallen, risen, floated off into its orbit, while

into the crater of its absence flowed
the greater tear known as the Pacific Ocean.
                                            So:
a story full of loss and eros, three-fifths
of the way to myth. Let's leave it there – something human,
homespun, like a basket, a translation, or a loaf of bread –
beside the incandescent water. Our cabin sat
under its little party hat of lights, and to it,
wanting its warmth, and supper, and to give our gifts,
we went.

ON LEAVING

Leaving home is the beginning of resemblance.
  – David Seymour

On leaving, you circulate among the things you own
to say farewell, properly,
knowing they will not cease to exist
after your departure, but go,
slowly, each in its own way,
wild.
So long and thanks, with one last chop, tap,
twiddle. It won't work just to
flip them into negatives – minus T-shirt, minus Roger
Tory Peterson both east and west –
nor to convert them into liquid
assets. This is no yard sale, this is loss,
whose interior is larger than its shell, the way you wish
home was. Do not dig the dog's bones up
nor the rosebush by the porch.
Choose a few companions of no weight –
a crow feather found in the parking lot,
the strawsmell of her hair, a few
books of the dead, *1000*
Best Loved Puns. And leave. There is a loneliness
which must be entered rather than resolved, the moon's
pull on the roof which made those asphalt shingles
shine. A time for this,
a time for that, a time to let them both escape into
whateverness, a time to cast

away stones, to stop
building and remembering and building artful
monuments upon the memories.

                              To leave.
To step off into darker darkness,
that no moon we call new.

ACKNOWLEDGEMENTS

I have, over the years, been fortunate in having excellent readers
attend to my work. Thanks to Roo Borson, Robert Bringhurst,
Barry Dempster, Stan Dragland, Dennis Lee, Tim Lilburn, and
Kim Maltman for this long-term listening. As always, I am espe-
cially indebted to Jan Zwicky.

Thanks also are due to the magazines, some still active, some
having passed on to little-mag heaven (where there ain't no typos
and the Canada Council makes house calls), that first printed
these poems, and have been perennial sustainers of poetry. I hope
this list (east to west) is reasonably complete: *TickleAce*, *The
Fiddlehead*, *Pottersfield Portfolio*, *Windhorse*, *Matrix*, *Quarry*,
Poetry Canada Review, *Arc*, *The Canadian Forum*, *Exile*, *Brick*,
Descant, *Saturday Night*, *Harvest*, *Impulse*, *Tics*, *Eclipse*,
Applegarth's Folly, *Stuffed Crocodile*, *Prairie Fire*, *Grain*,
Dandelion, *Event*, and *The Malahat Review*.

Among literary presses let me again thank the chapbook pub-
lishers – Reference West, Outlaw Editions, and Trout Lily – as
well as Brick Books, Coach House, and of course everyone at
McClelland & Stewart for supporting Canadian poetry over the
years. Special thanks to Ellen Seligman, Anita Chong, and Peter
Buck at M&S.

Some of these poems were written with particular people in mind.
Let me just mention "Bird Thou Never Wert" (John McKay),
"Simply Because Light" (Jean McKay), "Night Skating on the
Little Paddle River" (Bob Zwicky), "Suddenly, at home" (Naomi
McKay Sharpe), "Setting Up the Drums" (Andy Miller), "To

Danceland" (Margaret McKay), "Finger Pointing at the Moon" (Jane Clement Chamberlin), "Wings of Song" (Stan Dragland), and "Another Theory of Dusk" (Jan Zwicky).

A couple of these poems ("But Nature Has Her Darker Side" and "On Seeing the First Turkey Vultures of Spring") have sustained minor revisions. The prologue poem was written to introduce this book.

INDEX OF TITLES